S0-AWK-407

Grand Diplôme Cooking Course

Volume 16

Grand Diplôme Cooking Course

A Danbury Press Book

The Danbury Press

a division of Grolier Enterprises, Inc.

Robert B. Clarke   Publisher

This book has been adapted from the Grand Diplôme Cooking Course, originally published by Purnell Cookery, U.S.A.

Purnell Grand Diplôme Editorial Board

Rosemary Hume and Muriel Downes Principals, London Cordon Bleu Cookery School, England

Anne Willan	Editor
Eleanor Noderer	Associate Editor
Sheryl Julian	Assistant Editor
John Paton	Managing Editor
José Northey	Co-ordinating Editor
Peter Leather	Art Editor
Charles F. Turgeon	Wine Consultant

Library of Congress Catalog Card Number: 72-13896
© B.P.C. Publishing, 1971, and
© Phoebus Publishing, 1972.
Filmsetting by Petty and Sons Ltd., Leeds, England.
Printed in the United States of America

23456789987654

'Le Cordon Bleu, the Cordon Bleu School of Paris, the owner of the trademark and service mark ''Le Cordon Bleu'' registered in the United States and France and of the trade name ''Le Cordon Bleu'', is not connected with or sponsoring this publication.'

All recipes have been tested either at the Cordon Bleu Cookery School in London or in our U.S. test kitchens.

Note: all recipe quantities in this book serve 4 people unless otherwise stated.

Contents

Menus

A gourmet menu   8–15
Stuffed Artichokes Vinaigrette   10
Sweetbreads Tante Marie   12
Chicken à la Suisse   12
Pêches Melba   15

Spice pork for a change   40–45
Eggs Maryland   42
Spiced Pork Tenderloin   44
Fried Rice   44
Marinated Fruit Bowl   44

Prepare ahead for a party   74–81
Mushrooms in White Wine or Potage Vert   76–77
Chicken with Tuna   79
Galette Normande   80

Menus for many   102–109
Menu 1: Potage Pondicherry (Cream of Leek and Rice Soup) 104
         Vitello Tonnato   104
         Tangerine Mousse   104

Menu 2: Cacik (Turkish Yogurt Soup)   106
         Ballotines of Chicken with Prunes   106
         Praline Cream   107

Menu 3: Steak Flan with Zucchini Salad   109
         Strawberries Cardinal   109

Features
Shellfish (3)   16–23
Cooking for a Freezer   24–39
Japanese Cooking   46–58
Outdoor Entertaining   59–73
Hot Savory Molds   82–91
Preserves (3)   92–97
Homemade Vinegars   98–101
Spanish and Portuguese Cooking   110–129
Petits Fours   130–133
Cooking Curiosities   134–135
Index   137–141

From the Editor

Ice-cold gazpacho soup, saffron-flavored paella and colorful caldeirada with its cargo of freshly-caught fish are among the most famous dishes from Iberia, but in the **Cooking of Spain and Portugal** you'll discover many lesser known specialties like Spanish partridges in chocolate sauce and 'bacon from heaven', a meltingly rich Portuguese almond cake. Continue your world tour in Volume 16 of the Grand Diplôme Cooking Course and explore the delicate art of **Japanese Cooking**. Learn to appreciate the subtle harmonies of texture, color and flavor in recipes like norimaki sushi — specially cooked rice with fish, eggs and vegetables rolled in tissue-thin sheets of seaweed.

With the advice of the Cordon Bleu Cookery School in London, you can become skilled in making **Hot Savory Molds** from France that include melting mousselines made with chicken, fish or veal, and the famous quenelles — fluffy fish dumplings bathed in a rich creamy sauce. For superlative **Shellfish**, try the classic crab Armoricaine with brandy, mushrooms and white wine. Read the controversial history of lobster Américaine and sample the ever popular recipe of fresh lobster flamed in brandy, then sautéed with garlic, tomatoes and white wine.

Plan ahead for future feasting and follow the many helpful hints on **Cooking for the Freezer**. You'll find good advice on the practicalities of when to store and freeze fish, fowl, meat and sweet dishes, with delectable recipes designed especially for freezing. More traditional, but equally appealing, are the jams and marmalades made with fruits ranging from grapefruit to grapes in our third feature on **Preserves**. To finish a formal meal on a sweet note, try making a selection of delicious **Petits Fours** from the recipes included here.

The **Menus** in this Volume are as diverse as the features. Sweetbreads star in an elegant dinner, and pork is spiced for a tempting supper. Sweet-sour spareribs, stuffed barbecued lamb chops and sizzling char-grilled steaks are suggested in **Menus for Outdoor Entertaining** or, for an indoor gathering, follow one of three **Menus for Many** centered on veal, chicken, or steak in aspic. Bon Appétit!

Anne Willan

Sweetbreads Tante Marie with mushrooms are coated with sauce and served on croûtes

A GOURMET MENU

Stuffed Artichokes Vinaigrette

Sweetbreads Tante Marie
Green Beans   Boiled New Potatoes
or
Chicken à la Suisse

Peach Melba

~~

Red wine – Nuits St. Georges (Burgundy)
or Pinot Noir (California)

Here's a menu to delight a discriminating palate – globe artichokes, filled with a ham dressing, followed by sweetbreads in a mushroom and wine sauce or, if you prefer, chicken à la Suisse, made with noodles and cheese, and ending with the classic peach Melba.

In the heart of the Côte de Nuits – the northern half of Burgundy's 'Slope of Gold' – a red wine is produced that blends well with sweetbreads or chicken. Called Nuits St. Georges, after the town of that name, this wine offers an exceptional bouquet and a fine, firm flavor. The pinot noir grape in this wine is also raised in California and makes America's finest red wine in the Burgundy tradition.

9

TIMETABLE

Day before
Make or buy ice cream and store in the freezer. Make Melba sauce and chill.

Morning
Poach the peaches.
Trim and cook the artichokes. Prepare filling for artichokes but do not add ham. Chop the ham and store in plastic wrap to keep the color.
Blanch and press the sweetbreads; cut croûtes.
Line deep pan with bacon and sliced vegetables, ready for chicken.

Assemble equipment and ingredients for final cooking from 6:30 for dinner around 8 p.m.

You will find that **cooking times** given in the individual recipes for these dishes have sometimes been adapted in the timetable to help you when cooking and serving this menu as a party meal.

Order of Work
6:30
Start cooking sweetbreads, add wine and stock, cover and simmer. *Cook chicken.*
Whip Chantilly cream for peach Melba, flavor it and put into a pastry bag fitted with a star tube; store in refrigerator. Chill coupe or sherbet glasses.
6:45
Add ham to dressing for artichokes. Remove chokes, put artichokes on serving plates and spoon filling into the cavities.
7:00
Fry croûtes.
7:20
Cook potatoes *or noodles.*
Keep noodles in hot water when cooked and rinsed.
Finish sauce for sweetbreads, *or make sauce for chicken.*
Keep sweetbreads warm in the sauce.
7:40
Cook green beans and drain potatoes. Toss potatoes in melted butter and chopped parsley. Sauté mushrooms.
Drain noodles and toss in butter and pepper. Carve chicken, arrange pieces over noodles, add sauce and brown under broiler. Keep warm.
Heat croûtes in oven, arrange sweetbreads with mushrooms on a platter, cover and keep warm.
Drain and place green beans in serving dish.
8:00
Serve artichokes.
Complete peach Melba just before serving.

Appetizer

Stuffed Artichokes Vinaigrette

4 globe artichokes

For dressing
2 shallots, finely chopped
6 tablespoons olive oil
1 cup ($\frac{1}{4}$ lb) mushrooms, finely chopped
3 tablespoons white wine
2 tablespoons white wine vinegar
salt and pepper
squeeze of lemon juice (optional)
1 clove of garlic, crushed (optional)
$\frac{1}{2}$ cup finely chopped cooked ham
1 tablespoon chopped parsley or chopped mixed herbs

Method
Trim the tops and leaves of the artichokes with scissors and cut stalks level with base. Put artichokes into a kettle of boiling salted water and simmer about 35–40 minutes or until a leaf can be pulled out easily. Drain, refresh under cold running water, and let stand upside down until cold.

To make the dressing: sauté shallots slowly in 2 tablespoons of the oil until just tender. Stir in the mushrooms and cook 2–3 minutes or until moisture has evaporated. Transfer mixture to a bowl and stand until cool. Stir in the wine, vinegar and remaining oil. Season well with salt and pepper and add lemon juice if the filling is not tart enough. Flavor with a little garlic, if you like, and add the ham. Marinate 15–20 minutes to develop the flavor.

Prepare each artichoke by pulling out some of the center leaves until the choke can be reached. With a teaspoon or ball cutter scrape out all the hairy choke. Put a spoonful of dressing in the center cavity of each artichoke, set them on individual salad plates and sprinkle with chopped parsley or herbs. Serve cold.

Chopped shallots, mushrooms and ham are mixed with wine, vinegar and oil; the filling is marinated to develop the flavor

After some of the center leaves and the choke have been removed, the filling is spooned into the center cavity of the artichoke

Well-trimmed artichokes, stuffed with ham flavored with herbs, make good appetizers

Entrée

Sweetbreads Tante Marie

2–3 pairs of sweetbreads
1 cup veal or chicken stock
3 tablespoons oil
scant ½ cup butter
2 medium onions, quartered
2 cloves of garlic, split in half
salt and pepper
1 teaspoon flour
2 tablespoons brandy
¾ cup dry white wine
bouquet garni
2 cups (½ lb) small mushrooms
4–5 croûtes of bread
1 tablespoon tomato purée
a little kneaded butter (made
    with 2 tablespoons butter
    and 1 tablespoon flour)
½ cup heavy cream

Method

Prepare sweetbreads. Simmer them in the stock for 10 minutes, drain well and pat dry with paper towels. Reserve the stock in which they were cooked.

Heat oil and 3 tablespoons butter in a skillet, add onions and garlic, salt and pepper and cook over a fairly high heat, stirring frequently, for 2–3 minutes. Add sweetbreads and brown them, turning frequently. Sprinkle with flour; when well mixed, add brandy, heat it and flame. Add wine, reserved stock and bouquet garni. Bring to a boil, cover and simmer 40 minutes or until sweetbreads are very tender.

Trim mushroom stems level with bases of caps and sauté caps in 1 tablespoon butter. Set aside. Brown croûtes in remaining butter and arrange them in an ovenproof dish. Slice sweetbreads in half and place on the croûtes. Strain

liquid from pan into a clean pan and stir tomato purée into it, then add kneaded butter and cream. Bring this sauce to a boil, stirring, and add seasoning. Spoon over the sweetbreads and surround them with the mushrooms. Serve with green beans and small new potatoes tossed in butter and parsley.

Any ducts and skin must be removed from the sweetbreads before the final cooking

The sauce for sweetbreads Tante Marie is thickened with a little kneaded butter

To Prepare Sweetbreads

Soak them for several hours in salted water to which 1–2 slices of lemon or a few drops of vinegar have been added. Rinse sweetbreads, put in a pan and cover with water. Add a little salt and another slice of lemon; bring to a boil over low heat, skimming the top when necessary. Drain sweetbreads; rinse quickly in cold water. Remove any ducts and skin that will pull off easily. Press them between 2 flat plates, with a 2 lb weight on top, until cold.

Alternative entrée

Chicken à la Suisse

3½–4 lb roasting chicken, trussed
4 slices of bacon
1 large onion, thinly sliced
2 large carrots, thinly sliced
1 stalk of celery, thinly sliced
½ cup stock (made from chicken giblets)
bouquet garni
1 package (½ lb) noodles
2 tablespoons butter
black pepper, freshly ground
2 tablespoons grated Parmesan cheese

For cheese sauce
2 tablespoons butter
2 tablespoons flour
1½ cups milk (infused with 1 slice of onion, 5–6 peppercorns, blade of mace and ½ bay leaf)
½ cup grated Gruyère or Swiss cheese
salt and pepper
2–3 tablespoons heavy cream

Method

Lay bacon slices on the bottom of a deep flameproof pan, cover with onion, carrots and celery and put the whole chicken on top. Cover and cook over a low heat for 10–15 minutes. Pour stock over chicken, tuck in bouquet garni with vegetables, cover and cook gently, either over direct heat or in a moderate oven (350°F) for about 50–60 minutes.

Put the noodles into a large pan of boiling salted water, reduce heat a little and cook 10 minutes or until they are just tender. Drain them, rinse under hot running water and return to the rinsed pan with 1 cup hot water.

To make the cheese sauce: melt butter in a saucepan, take from heat and stir in the flour until smooth. Pour on the milk and cook, stirring constantly, until the sauce thickens. Simmer 2 minutes. Take from the heat, beat in the grated Gruyère or Swiss cheese, a little at a time, and taste for seasoning. Add the cream and keep the sauce warm.

Remove the chicken from the pan to a carving board or platter, and reduce liquid in pan a little; strain, discarding vegetables and flavorings. Skim fat from surface and add liquid to cheese sauce.

Drain noodles; heat them in the butter, adding plenty of freshly ground pepper. Pour noodles into a hot flameproof serving dish. Carve chicken into pieces and arrange them on top of the noodles. Coat chicken pieces with sauce and sprinkle the top with grated Parmesan cheese. Brown the dish lightly under the broiler.

Chicken à la Suisse is coated with a cheese sauce before being lightly browned

Peach Melba, a dish created by the chef Escoffier, is topped with Chantilly cream

Peach Melba is made with fresh peaches, raspberries, vanilla ice cream and Chantilly cream

Dessert

Pêches Melba
(Peach Melba)

4 ripe peaches
¼ cup sugar
1 cup water
½ vanilla bean
1 pint vanilla ice cream
½ cup Chantilly cream

For Melba sauce
1 pint fresh red raspberries or
   1 package frozen raspberries
   (thawed)
2 tablespoons confectioners'
   sugar (or to taste)

4 coupe or sherbet glasses;
pastry bag and star tube

The peaches should be ripe. To test, rub skin gently with the blade of a table knife — if ripe, the skin peels off easily; if not, do not scald them but simply cut in half and poach with skin on. When cooked, let cool and skin peels easily.

Method
Heat sugar, water and vanilla bean until sugar has dissolved; boil 5 minutes to make a syrup. Peel peaches, if ripe, halve them, removing pits, and put rounded side down in the syrup. Poach over low heat about 10 minutes, frequently spooning syrup over the peaches, until they are tender but still keep their shape.

Let peaches cool in syrup (peel less ripe ones) and then drain. Prepare Melba sauce by rubbing raspberries through a nylon sieve, or purée in a blender and strain to remove seeds. Beat confectioners' sugar into the purée a little at a time and chill. Frozen raspberries need very little sugar.

To serve, put a scoop of

vanilla ice cream in each coupe or sherbet glass, arrange two peach halves over it, coat with a little Melba sauce and decorate with a rosette of Chantilly cream.

Chantilly Cream
Whip ½ cup heavy cream until it starts to thicken; add ½ tablespoon sugar and ¼ teaspoon vanilla; continue beating until the cream holds a shape.

Peach Melba was created by the 'Emperor of chefs', Escoffier, for the famous soprano Dame Nellie Melba. However, when first served, the dessert consisted simply of fresh poached peaches on a bed of vanilla ice cream.

Perhaps the dessert earned its reputation because it was served on a swan carved from a block of ice. Escoffier himself did not think much of the dish until years later when he added the spoonful of raspberry purée that gives peach Melba its distinctive character.

SHELLFISH (3)

When cooked in the classic style with brandy, wine and cream, few foods can rival shellfish for sheer unbridled luxury. This last feature on shellfish includes a number of sophisticated dishes worthy of the grandest occasions. Simpler recipes were given in Volumes 3 and 10.

Lobster Margareta

4 live lobsters (1–1½ lb each)
2 quarts court bouillon (see box)
2 shallots, finely chopped
2 tablespoons butter
½ cup sherry
2 cups (½ lb) mushrooms, sliced
juice of ½ lemon
salt and pepper
4 tomatoes, peeled, seeded and cut in 8 pieces
¼ cup heavy cream
watercress (to garnish)

For sauce
3 tomatoes, peeled, seeded and finely chopped or ¼ cup tomato purée
2 cups mayonnaise (made with lemon juice instead of vinegar)
2 teaspoons Dijon-style mustard
1 tablespoon chopped mixed herbs (parsley, tarragon, chervil)
pinch of cayenne
few drops of Worcestershire sauce
squeeze of lemon juice (optional)

Method

In a covered kettle boil the live lobsters in court bouillon for 12–15 minutes, cool a little in the liquid, then drain lobsters and cool completely.

Cook the shallots in the butter until soft but not browned, add the sherry and simmer until reduced by half. Add the mushrooms and lemon juice, season and cook quickly for 2–3 minutes or until mushrooms are tender. Add the tomatoes and cream, simmer 2 minutes longer or until the tomatoes are just cooked; taste for seasoning and cool.

Split cooked lobsters in half lengthwise, remove the tail meat and cut it in thick slices or 'scallops', discarding the dark intestinal tract. Crack the claws and remove the meat from them and the legs and the body, discarding the head sac.

Spread the mushroom mixture in the bottom of each lobster shell and arrange the lobster meat on top, placing the claw meat in the body shell.

To make the sauce: mix the tomatoes or tomato purée with the mayonnaise, add the mustard, chopped herbs, cayenne and Worcestershire sauce and taste for seasoning, adding a little lemon juice if necessary.

Coat each lobster half with sauce and serve the rest separately.

Arrange the lobsters on a large platter or on individual plates and garnish with watercress. Serve with cold boiled rice, mixed with vinaigrette dressing.

Court Bouillon for Shellfish

For 2 quart quantity: in a kettle large enough to hold the shellfish, melt 2 tablespoons butter and cook 4 sliced onions and 2 sliced carrots until soft. Add the juice of 1 lemon, a large bouquet garni, 12 peppercorns, 2 quarts water, 1½ cups white wine and ½ teaspoon salt. Then simmer 15–20 minutes; strain before using.

Lobster Pilaf

2 live lobsters (1–1½ lb each) or 1 live lobster (2½–3 lb)
2 quarts court bouillon
6 tablespoons butter
béchamel sauce, made with 3 tablespoons butter, 3 tablespoons flour, 2 cups milk (infused with slice of onion, 6 peppercorns, blade of mace and bay leaf)
1 teaspoon paprika
¼ cup sherry
4 egg yolks
1½ cups heavy cream

For pilaf
1 cup rice
3 tablespoons butter
1 medium onion, finely chopped
2–2½ cups stock
salt and pepper
pinch of saffron, soaked in 2 tablespoons boiling water for 30 minutes

Ring mold (1 quart capacity)

Method

Set oven at moderate (350°F) and lightly butter the mold.

To make pilaf: in a flameproof casserole melt 2 tablespoons of the butter, add the onion and cook gently until soft but not brown. Add the rice and fry 2–3 minutes, stirring, until the grains look transparent. Add 2 cups stock, season and add the saffron liquid. Bring to a boil, cover and bake in heated oven for 15 minutes. Add more stock if the pan looks dry and continue cooking 5–7 minutes or until the rice is tender. Let stand, covered, for 10 minutes.

To cook the lobsters: in a large covered kettle boil live lobsters in court bouillon for 12–15 minutes and drain them. Remove the tails, cut along the membrane underneath and extract the meat in one piece; cut the meat into thick slices or 'scallops', discarding the dark intestinal tract. Split the body shells lengthwise and scrape out the soft body meat and any coral, discarding the head sac. Mix the coral and soft body meat with ¼ cup of the butter, rub through a fine strainer and reserve. Crack the claws and extract the meat from them and the legs.

Make the béchamel sauce and keep warm.

Add the remaining tablespoon of butter for the pilaf to the rice, stir it in with a fork and put the rice in the mold, pressing it down lightly; keep warm.

Melt the remaining 2 tablespoons butter, add the paprika and cook very gently for 1 minute. Add all the remaining lobster meat and sherry and heat very carefully.

Watchpoint: if the lobster meat is heated too much, it will toughen.

Stir the egg yolks and cream together and stir into the béchamel sauce. Add the sauce to the lobster and cook over low heat, stirring carefully, until the sauce thickens slightly. Do not boil it. Add the lobster butter in small pieces and shake the pan over low heat until the butter is absorbed.

Unmold the rice onto a platter and fill the center with the lobster mixture. Spoon remaining lobster mixture around the mold or serve in a separate dish.

Lobster Boréale

2 live hen lobsters
(1–1½ lb each)
2 quarts court bouillon
(see box)
6 tablespoons butter
béchamel sauce, made with
3 tablespoons butter,
2 tablespoons flour, 1½ cups
milk (infused with slice of
onion, 6 peppercorns, blade
of mace and bay leaf)

For fish mousseline
1 lb white fish fillets (pike,
haddock or other firm white
fish)
2 egg whites, lightly beaten
1 cup heavy cream
¼ cup milk
salt and pepper

For garnish
1 cup (¼ lb) mushrooms,
sliced
½ tablespoon butter
1 cup (½ lb) cooked, peeled
baby shrimps
4 hard-cooked eggs

*Oval mold or baking dish
(3 cup capacity)*

It is important to use hen lobsters for this recipe so their coral can color the sauce. To select a female lobster, look at the 2 small feelers under the body at the junction of the main shell and tail; in a hen lobster these feelers are soft and feathery, in a cock lobster they are firm.

Method

In a large covered kettle boil the live lobsters in the court bouillon for 12–15 minutes. Drain them, reserving the court bouillon, and cut them in half lengthwise. Remove the tail meat and cut it in thick slices or 'scallops', discarding the dark intestinal tract. Crack claws of 1 lobster only and extract meat. The other claws and shell are kept intact for garnish, and may be eaten later.

Set oven at moderate (350°F) and butter the mold or dish.

To make fish mousseline: remove any bones and skin from the fish, pass flesh twice through the fine blade of a grinder and pound in a mortar and pestle until smooth. Gradually work in the lightly beaten egg whites, then work the mixture through a wire sieve. Or, instead of pounding and sieving, work fish with the egg whites in a blender for a few seconds.

Gradually beat in the cream, then the milk and season the mixture well. If the mixture is at all soft, a little salt will stiffen it at once. If the kitchen is hot, put the mixture in a metal bowl over a bowl of ice to chill it thoroughly while working in the egg whites and cream.

Spoon the mixture into the prepared mold or dish, cover with foil and cook in a water bath in heated oven for 30–35 minutes or until mixture is firm to the touch. Let stand 5 minutes before turning out.

To make lobster butter: remove the coral and soft body meat, discarding the head sac, and pound with the butter, then work through a sieve.

Meanwhile make béchamel sauce, beat in lobster butter, piece by piece, and thin sauce, if necessary, with a little reserved court bouillon so it just coats back of a wooden spoon. Keep warm in a water bath.

Watchpoint: do not bring sauce to a boil after lobster butter is added or it will separate.

To prepare the garnish: cook the mushrooms with seasoning in the butter over

Ingredients for lobster boréale (see also photograph of finished dish on page 20) include mushrooms, eggs, cream, milk and a firm white fish such as pike

low heat until just tender. Mix them with the shrimps. Cut the hard-cooked eggs in half lengthwise, scoop out the yolks and work the yolks through a sieve. Fill the egg white halves with the shrimp and mushroom mixture.

To serve, unmold the mousseline onto a flat, oval platter, arrange lobster meat, overlapping, on top and spoon over the lobster sauce. Arrange the stuffed eggs around the platter and warm it carefully in a moderate oven (350°F) for 3–5 minutes. Sprinkle the sieved egg yolks on top of the eggs. Decorate with the reserved lobster shells, split and brushed lightly with oil so they shine.

Lobster Boréale is garnished with a split lobster shell, lightly brushed with oil to make it shine (recipe is on page 19)

Lobster Américaine

2 live lobsters (1½–1¾ lb each)
3 tablespoons oil
5 tablespoons brandy
¼ cup butter
1 medium onion, finely chopped
2 cloves of garlic, crushed
4 tomatoes, peeled, seeded and finely chopped
1 cup white wine
salt and pepper
1 cup each of cooked diced green beans, turnips and carrots
½ cup stock (optional)
3 tablespoons flour
2 teaspoons tomato paste

Method

To kill live lobsters with a knife: lay each one in turn flat on a board, hard shell up, with the head facing to the right, tail to the left; cover the tail with a cloth. Hold the lobster firmly behind the head with your left hand and with the point of a sharp knife, pierce down to the board through the cross mark that lies on center. of the head. The lobster is killed at once. Continue splitting the lobster body as far as the tail, then cut the tail from the body in 1 piece. Repeat this with the other lobster.

Discard the head sacs and scoop out the soft meat and any coral from the bodies of the lobsters and reserve.

Cut the lobster tails (including the shells) into thick slices or 'scallops', discarding the intestinal tract. Crack claws.

Heat the oil, add the pieces of lobster tail and claws in the shell and sauté gently, shell side down, until the shells start to turn red. Flame with brandy. Take lobster pieces and claws from pan; reserve.

Add half the butter and the onion and garlic to pan and cook gently until soft but not brown. Add the chopped tomatoes, wine and seasoning and simmer gently for 10 minutes. Add the diced vegetables with a little stock if tomatoes are not very juicy.

To make lobster butter: work remaining butter to a smooth paste with the soft lobster body meat, any coral, flour and tomato paste and rub through a nylon strainer. Take the pan from the heat and add the lobster butter a small piece at a time, shaking the pan until the butter is absorbed. Bring the mixture back to a boil and simmer gently 1 minute.

Extract the meat from the lobster claws. Snip the soft underside of the shell on each piece of tail meat so the flesh can be removed easily when eating; return the pieces in the shell to pan with claw meat. Reheat carefully, taste for seasoning, transfer to a dish and serve with boiled rice.

The name **lobster Américaine** is the subject of incessant gastronomic debate. Many experts insist that the true title should be **Armoricaine**, arguing that the dish originated in Armorica, the Roman name for Brittany. Others insist that lobster Américaine was created by a Parisian chef named Pierre Fraisse, born in Provence, which might account for typically Provençal ingredients in the dish — tomatoes, oil and garlic.

Crab Armoricaine comes from Brittany. In the 17th century the main port of the region, Nantes, was a center for the spice trade; therefore, many local recipes are spiced.

Crab Armoricaine

1½ lb backfin crab meat
1 large onion, finely chopped
3 tablespoons butter
2 cups (½ lb) mushrooms, chopped
2 tablespoons brandy
1 large tomato, peeled, seeded and crushed to a pulp
½ cup white wine
salt and pepper
pinch of cayenne
pinch of curry powder
2 tablespoons browned breadcrumbs
2–3 tablespoons melted butter

Method

Cook the onion in the butter until soft but not brown. Add the mushrooms and continue cooking for 2–3 minutes or until the moisture has evaporated. Add the brandy, crushed tomato, wine, seasoning and spices and stir in the crab meat.

Transfer the mixture to a baking dish, scatter with breadcrumbs and sprinkle with melted butter. Before serving, brown the crab mixture in a hot oven (425°F) for about 7–10 minutes, or under the broiler.

Simple Mustard Sauce

1 tablespoon Dijon-style mustard
4 tablespoons butter
1 tablespoon flour
1 cup boiling water
few drops of lemon juice
salt and pepper

Makes 1 cup.

Method

In a large saucepan melt 1 tablespoon of the butter and stir in the flour, off the heat. Whisk in the boiling water in a steady stream and continue beating until smooth. Stir in remaining butter, in pieces.

Add a few drops of lemon juice and the mustard and season to taste. Pour into a sauce boat and serve hot.

Crab Croquettes

1 lb crab meat
thick béchamel sauce, made with ¼ cup butter, 3 tablespoons flour, 1½ cups milk (infused with slice of onion, 6 peppercorns, blade of mace and bay leaf)
1 large egg
salt and pepper
few drops of Tabasco
fried parsley (for garnish) – optional

For coating
½ cup seasoned flour (made with ½ teaspoon salt and large pinch of pepper)
2 eggs beaten to mix
½ cup dry white breadcrumbs
deep fat (for frying)

These croquettes make excellent cocktail hors d'œuvre.

Method

Make béchamel sauce and leave until cold. Beat in the crab meat with the egg, salt, pepper and Tabasco to taste.

If necessary, chill the mixture until firm and shape into balls the size of walnuts. Roll the balls in seasoned flour, then brush with beaten egg and roll in breadcrumbs.

Heat the deep fat to 360°F on a fat thermometer and fry the croquettes until golden brown.

Watchpoint: do not fry too many at once; they should not touch each other.

Drain croquettes on paper towels and serve very hot with mustard sauce. If you like, garnish with fried parsley.

Curried Shrimps

1½ lb uncooked, unpeeled
  jumbo shrimps
1 quart court bouillon (for
  poaching) – see box on
  page 18

For curry cream sauce
1 tablespoon curry powder
¼ cup heavy cream
1 large onion, chopped
3 tablespoons butter
1 tablespoon flour
1½ teaspoons tomato paste
1½ cups veal or chicken stock
1 tablespoon red currant jelly
¼ cup coconut milk (see box)
juice of ½ lemon

For accompaniments
1 cup rice, boiled
grated fresh coconut or
  unsweetened shredded
  coconut
currants or raisins, soaked
  overnight in water to cover,
  slowly brought to a boil,
  simmered 3–4 minutes and
  drained
fresh or canned crushed
  pineapple, drained and
  mixed with chopped candied
  ginger

A simpler version of this recipe was given in Volume 3.

Method
To make the curry cream sauce: cook onion in the butter over low heat until soft but not browned. Add curry powder and continue to cook gently for 3–4 minutes, stirring occasionally. Stir in flour and tomato paste, pour on stock and bring sauce to a boil, stirring. Cover and simmer 8–12 minutes. Take from heat, add red currant jelly, coconut milk and lemon juice and stir until jelly is melted. Simmer 5–7 minutes longer and keep warm.

In a kettle poach the shrimps in court bouillon for 4–5 minutes or until just cooked. Cool a little, drain and peel them.

Take the curry sauce from the heat and stir in the cream. Pour into a serving dish and pile the shrimps on top. Serve hot with the accompaniments in separate bowls.

Coconut Milk
If milk from a fresh coconut is not available, pour ½ cup boiling water over ¼ cup unsweetened shredded coconut and let stand 15 minutes. Strain through cheesecloth, squeezing to extract all the coconut milk liquid.

Fish Stock
For 1 quart: blanch 1 large onion, peeled and sliced; drain and refresh. Melt 1 tablespoon butter in a large saucepan, add onion and 1 lb washed fish bones, cover and cook slowly for 5 minutes. Add 1 carrot, peeled and sliced, 1 stalk of celery, sliced, 5 cups water, bouquet garni, ½ teaspoon salt, 6 peppercorns, ½ cup dry white wine and a slice of lemon. Simmer gently, uncovered, for 20 minutes; strain and measure.

Shrimps Gourmet

1½ lb uncooked, peeled large
  shrimps
3 tablespoons butter
salt and pepper
few drops of Tabasco

For white wine sauce
velouté sauce, made with
    2 tablespoons butter,
    2 tablespoons flour and
    1½ cups fish stock
¾ cup white wine
2 shallots, finely chopped
3 tablespoons butter
3 egg yolks
¼ cup heavy cream
squeeze of lemon juice

For garnish
1 lb fresh asparagus or
    1 package frozen asparagus
3 tablespoons butter
1 cup (¼ lb) mushrooms, sliced
4 medium tomatoes, peeled,
    seeded and quartered

Method
To make white wine sauce: make velouté sauce and reserve. Simmer the shallot in the wine until the liquid is reduced by half. Soften 1½ tablespoons butter and work in the egg yolks. Strain in reduced wine, return mixture to the pan and cook in a water bath, stirring constantly, until slightly thickened. Work in remaining butter a little at a time, then take from heat and stir in cream and lemon juice. Stir in the reserved velouté sauce and heat gently without boiling; taste for seasoning and keep warm in a water bath.

To prepare garnish: if using fresh asparagus, wash well and snap stalks, discarding tough ends. With a vegetable peeler, peel the stalks.

Tie stalks in a bundle and stand them in a deep saucepan, green tips pointing up, in 2 inches boiling salted water so the tips cook in the steam and the stalks in the water. Cover and cook for 10–12 minutes or until the green tips are just tender; drain, refresh and drain again. Cook frozen asparagus according to package directions, drain, refresh and drain again.

Melt butter for garnish and cook mushrooms until tender. Add tomatoes and sauté 1–2 minutes or until just cooked. Add asparagus, heat garnish thoroughly, add seasoning and keep warm.

In a skillet or flameproof casserole melt the 3 tablespoons butter, add shrimps with salt, pepper and Tabasco, cover and cook gently on top of stove or in hot oven (400°F) for 5–7 minutes or until shrimps are just cooked, turning them once.

Arrange shrimps in a gratin or heatproof serving dish, spoon over garnish and coat with sauce. Brown lightly under broiler before serving.

Shrimps gourmet, garnished with tomatoes, asparagus and mushrooms, are coated with white wine sauce

Scallops Paimpolaise

$1\frac{1}{2}$ lb sea scallops
1 cup white wine
1 cup water
1 bay leaf
6 peppercorns
velouté sauce (made with
    3 tablespoons butter,
    $2\frac{1}{2}$ tablespoons flour, 2 cups
    liquid from cooking scallops,
    $\frac{1}{2}$ cup heavy cream)
$\frac{1}{4}$ cup grated Parmesan cheese

For duxelles mixture
3 cups ($\frac{3}{4}$ lb) mushrooms,
    finely chopped
3 tablespoons butter
3 shallots, finely chopped
1 tablespoon chopped parsley
1 teaspoon thyme or marjoram
salt and pepper

*4 large scallop shells or
    individual gratin dishes*

Method

To make duxelles mixture: melt the butter, add the shallots and cook gently until soft but not brown. Add the mushrooms and cook over high heat, stirring occasionally, until all the moisture has evaporated. Take from the heat, stir in the herbs and season to taste. Spread the duxelles mixture in the scallop shells or gratin dishes.

Mix the wine, water, bay leaf and peppercorns and bring to a boil. Add the scallops and simmer 4–5 minutes or until the scallops are just tender and the center is no longer transparent.

Drain and halve the scallops, reserving the cooking liquid, arrange them on top of the duxelles mixture in the shells or gratin dishes and keep warm.

Make the velouté sauce, using the strained, reserved cooking liquid, simmer 2 minutes, stir in cream, bring back to a boil. Take from the heat, add half the cheese and season to taste.

To serve, spoon sauce over scallops, sprinkle with remaining cheese and brown for about 5–7 minutes in a hot oven (425°F) or under broiler.

23

COOKING FOR A FREEZER

A freezer can do much more than just act as a long-term storage center for meat, fruit and vegetables. Using a freezer, you can plan ahead for parties so that very little last minute preparation is needed; you can save time — and often money — by doubling a recipe and freezing half of it. Unexpected guests will be no problem when you have a good supply of frozen dishes that are ready to heat and serve.

A surprisingly wide range of dishes are suitable for freezing. Soups, stews, casseroles, crêpes and dishes with a sauce freeze excellently as the high water content counteracts any tendency to dryness. Breads and pastry can be frozen baked or unbaked and most cakes, cookies and desserts like meringues emerge as though freshly made. Some fruits and vegetables — like peaches, tomatoes, mushrooms and zucchini — that cannot be frozen because their texture spoils, are fine when cooked and then frozen.

The dishes whose textures are spoiled by freezing are listed on the next page. Also there are foods that are hardly worth freezer space — unbaked cake batter, for example, freezes well but baked cakes can be stored for a much longer time. You can also freeze crêpe and pancake batter but it takes very little time to make the batter in the first place.

Nothing is improved by freezing; foods that cook quickly waste freezer space (unless they are left over). Fish and shellfish dishes are best freshly cooked; fish sauces, on the other hand, can take a long time to make and are well worth freezing.

How you fill your freezer is up to you — the following chart gives some suggestions for dishes to freeze but many other recipes already given in the Course can also be frozen. Detailed instructions on freezing uncooked and cooked foods, freezer wraps and containers were given in Volume 6 so a brief summary of only the most important points is included on page 27.

COOKED FOODS THAT FREEZE WELL

TYPE OF FOOD	TYPE OF DISH	STORAGE TIME
Meat, Poultry & Fish	Braised dishes with sauce	3 months
	Casseroles with sauce	2–3 months
	Pot roast with gravy	1–2 months
	Stews	3 months
	Sautéed dishes with sauce	2–3 months
Fruits & Vegetables	Cooked fruits (whole, sliced or puréed)	8–12 months
	Uncooked fruits (see Volume 6)	9–12 months
	Cooked vegetables (whole, sliced or puréed)	(see Volume 6)
	Uncooked vegetables	(see Volume 6)
Breads & Rolls	Biscuits (baked)	2–3 months
	Muffins (baked)	2–3 months
	Quick breads (baked)	3–4 months
	Coffeecakes (baked)	6–8 months
	(unbaked dough)	2 weeks
	Yeast breads (baked)	3–6 months
	(unbaked dough)	2 weeks
Cookies, Cakes & Pastries	Angel food and sponge cakes (baked)	3–4 months
	Fruit cakes (will keep 6–8 months without freezing)	—
	Pastry (baked pie shells etc.)	6 months
	(unbaked dough)	3 months
	Cookies (baked)	8–12 months
	(unbaked)	3 months
	Rich gâteaux and cakes (unfrosted and unfilled)	3 months
	(frosted or filled, but not with whipped cream)	2 months
	Rich pastries (baked, but not with whipped cream)	2 months
	Petits fours (baked, but not with whipped cream)	2 months
Ice Cream & Sherbets	Sherbet (homemade)	2–4 weeks
	Ice creams (homemade)	4–6 weeks
	Iced desserts and parfaits (homemade)	2–3 months
Miscellaneous	Crêpes (filled)	2–3 months
	(unfilled)	3 months
	Sauces (but not with egg yolks and cream)	3–4 months
	Soups (but not with egg yolks and cream)	3–4 months
	Pizza (baked)	2–3 months
	(unbaked)	1–2 weeks
	Savory molds and quenelles without sauce	1–2 months
	with sauce (but not with egg yolks and cream in sauce)	2–3 months
	Rice dishes (use only converted rice)	2–3 months

Note: as some commercially-prepared frozen foods contain stabilizers they may keep longer in the freezer than the same food cooked at home.

COOKED FOODS THAT DO NOT FREEZE WELL

1 Hard-cooked egg whites toughen.

2 Aspic and gelatin molds crystallize, then liquefy when thawed.

3 Dishes with very smooth textures like egg custard will curdle; sauces enriched with egg yolks and cream tend to separate; a stabilizer such as flour, cornstarch or gelatin helps prevent this.

4 Foods like cooked meats and chicken without sauce tend to become stringy and tasteless.

5 Deep fried foods lose crispness.

6 Pasta sticks together unless layered with sauce. Converted rice freezes better than regular or quick cooking kinds.

7 Cooked potatoes in a sauce become soft, though French fries or stuffed baked potatoes freeze quite well.

DO NOT FREEZE

1 Whipped cream in large quantities as it will separate.

2 Glacé and fondant icings (on cakes).

3 Cooked leftovers once they have been thawed.

4 Do not use foil containers when freezing mixtures containing vinegar as metal may affect the flavor.

Points to remember

1 Color, flavor, texture and nutritive value of food are affected if it is stored at temperatures above 0°F or if put to freeze at above −5°F.

2 Freeze food quickly to prevent large ice crystals from forming and damaging texture.

3 Do not try to freeze too much food at once or the temperature of the freezer will not stay low enough to freeze the food quickly; when frozen, food can be packed tightly.

4 Thaw food slowly, preferably in the refrigerator.

5 Thickened liquids tend to thicken more when frozen, so prepare sauces slightly thinner than usual.

6 If possible add cream or egg yolks to sauces and soups after thawing. Otherwise reheat them in a double boiler, stirring often to prevent separation.

7 Some seasonings taste stronger after freezing; use salt, pepper and garlic sparingly. Others lose flavor such as cinnamon, chili, onion and soy sauce.

8 Seal all packages tightly as flavors, particularly of cooked foods, are easily transferred. White patches called 'freezer burns' (from oxidation and evaporation) will form on foods that are not airtight.

9 Freezing does not preserve food indefinitely so refer to the charts in Volume 6 and opposite for recommended maximum storage times — after these recommended times, flavor and texture begin to deteriorate though the food will still be safe to eat.

To Wrap Cooked Dishes

Line the dish you will use for reheating the food with foil and arrange cooked food in it. Cover and freeze. When solid, lift foil-wrapped food from dish, seal in freezer wrap, freezing bag or carton and replace in freezer. Or, instead of lining dish with foil, food can be released by placing dish upside down under hot running water until frozen block of food falls from it.

Place cakes on plates or rounds of cardboard before wrapping to freeze so the cake is less likely to be damaged. Leave pie shells and other fragile items in their pans.

Freeze large quantities of liquids like soup or stock in small containers or ice trays so a little can be used at a time. Separate items such as crêpes with sheets of wax paper so they do not stick together.

To Thaw Frozen Foods

With the exception of unbaked bread doughs, all foods thaw best in the refrigerator as slowly as possible (unless a commercial package states otherwise). Allow 12 hours for small packages, 24–36 hours for large roasts and casseroles. Cook vegetables (except corn on the cob) straight from the freezer.

Foods thaw twice as quickly at room temperature. They can be thawed even more quickly by placing watertight packages under cool running water or surrounding dishes or foil containers with warm water or heating gently on top of stove or in oven, but none of these procedures is advisable except in an emergency.

Seafood Pie

½ lb flounder fillet, cut in strips
½ lb sea scallops
½ lb cooked lobster meat
½ lb cooked, peeled medium shrimps
1 cup white wine
court bouillon (made with
   1 cup water, slice of onion,
   ½ carrot, sliced,
   6 peppercorns, bouquet
   garni, 1 whole clove,
   1 tablespoon lemon juice)
3 tablespoons butter
3 tablespoons flour
1 cup light cream
salt and pepper
pinch of nutmeg
flaky pastry (made with
   2 cups flour, pinch of salt,
   6 tablespoons shortening,
   6 tablespoons butter,
   8–10 tablespoons ice
   water)
1 egg, beaten to mix
   (for glaze)

Deep 9–10 inch pie dish

Method
Make the pastry dough and chill it.

Boil the white wine until it is reduced by half. Put the flounder in a shallow pan, pour over the wine and strained court bouillon, cover and poach about 1 minute or until the flounder just flakes easily. Lift it out with a slotted spoon and set aside.

Cut the scallops in 2–3 pieces, add them to the liquid and poach for 3–4 minutes or until just cooked; drain, set aside, reserving cooking liquid. Add the lobster meat and shrimps to the flounder and scallops and spread in dish.

In a saucepan melt the butter, stir in the flour and cook until straw-colored. Pour in the reserved cooking liquid from fish and bring to a boil, stirring. Simmer 2 minutes, add the cream and bring back to a boil. Take from the heat, season to taste with salt, pepper and nutmeg and pour over the fish.

Roll the pastry dough to a circle, cut a strip and set it around the pie dish on the flat edge. Press it down well and brush with water. Lift the rest of the dough with a rolling pin and lay it carefully over the dish. Trim around edge and seal or flute edges of dough with back of a knife, to help them rise, then indent them.

Roll out dough trimmings and cut leaves for decoration. With the point of a knife, make a hole in the center of the pie to allow steam to escape and arrange leaves around it. Chill and freeze.

Remove the pie from pie dish, wrap tightly and store in freezer.

To serve: replace pie in the pie dish, thaw and brush the pie with beaten egg to glaze. Bake in a hot oven (425°F) for 25–30 minutes or until pastry is well browned.

The finished terrine of duck is surrounded by some of the ingredients that go into it

Terrine of Duck

2 medium ducks (3½–4 lb each)
1 lb ground pork or veal
½ lb calves' or pigs' liver, ground
black pepper, freshly ground
½ teaspoon ground allspice
¼ cup port or sherry
1 medium onion, finely chopped
salt and pepper
1 bay leaf
rind of ½ orange, thinly peeled and cut in strips
luting paste (see box)—optional

To finish
2–3 slices of orange
½ cup aspic

Terrine or soufflé dish (2 quart capacity)

Method
Remove and discard the skin from the ducks. Cut off the breast meat and cut it into strips. Sprinkle with pepper and allspice, pour over the port or sherry and let marinate.

Remove the remaining duck meat from the carcass and grind it. Mix with the ground pork or veal, liver and onion and work together until smooth. Stir in the marinade from the breast meat and season well.

Fill the ground mixture into the terrine or soufflé dish in layers with the breast meat, beginning and ending with ground mixture. Smooth the surface, press the bay leaf and orange rind on top, add the terrine lid and seal with luting paste. If using a soufflé dish, cover the top tightly with foil.

Set terrine or dish in a water bath and bake in a moderately low oven (325°F) for 1–1½ hours or until firm to the touch and a skewer inserted in the terrine for 1 minute is hot to the touch when withdrawn. Let stand until cool, then remove the lid or foil, set a plate or board with a 2 lb weight on top and chill.

Turn out, wrap it tightly and freeze.

To serve: replace in terrine or dish and thaw. Remove bay leaf and orange rind and decorate top with orange slices, spoon over cool but still liquid aspic and chill until set. Serve as an appetizer or as an entrée with Belgian endive and orange salad.

Luting paste is a flour and water mixture used to seal terrines. To make it: stir 6–7 tablespoons water into 1 cup flour with a teaspoon or your forefinger to form a paste. Do not stir too much or paste will become elastic and shrink during cooking. Spread with the fingers, pressing well into the gap between terrine and lid.

Terrine of Chicken

3½–4 lb roasting chicken
1 cup (½ lb) chopped cooked tongue
8 thin slices of cooked ham
salt and pepper
pinch of ground mace or nutmeg
squeeze of lemon juice
1 cup fresh white breadcrumbs
1 small onion, finely chopped
½ teaspoon chopped sage
1 egg yolk
¼ cup chicken stock
luting paste (see box)—optional

Terrine or soufflé dish (1½–2 quart capacity)

Method
Remove and discard the skin from the chicken. Cut off the breast meat and slice it thinly. Sprinkle the slices with seasoning, mace or nutmeg, and a squeeze of lemon juice and reserve.

Cut the remaining meat from the chicken carcass and grind it with the tongue. Add the breadcrumbs, onion and sage and season to taste. Mix together the egg yolk and stock and stir into the chicken mixture a little at a time.

Line the terrine or soufflé dish with the sliced ham. Cut any that remains in strips and add it to the sliced chicken breast. Fill the dish with alternate layers of ground chicken mixture and sliced chicken and ham, beginning and ending with ground mixture. Add the terrine lid and seal with luting paste or cover the soufflé dish tightly with foil.

Place terrine or dish in a water bath and bake in a moderately low oven (325°F) for 1–1½ hours or until the mixture is firm to the touch and a skewer inserted in the center of the terrine for 1 minute is hot to the touch when withdrawn. Cool in the terrine or dish, then uncover it, set a plate or board with a 2 lb weight on top and chill.

Turn out the terrine, wrap tightly and freeze.

To serve: replace in terrine or dish and thaw. Serve as an appetizer or as an entrée with celery, apple and walnut salad.

Spiced Chicken

3–3½ lb roasting chicken, cut in pieces
1½ teaspoons ground cumin
1 teaspoon ground allspice
¼ teaspoon ground nutmeg
salt and pepper
1 tablespoon flour
¼ cup butter
12–16 small onions, blanched
1 tablespoon tomato paste
1½ cups chicken stock

Method
Mix the spices with salt and pepper and rub well into the chicken pieces; sprinkle them with flour.

In a flameproof casserole or skillet, melt butter and fry onions gently until browned. Take them from the pan, add chicken pieces, skin side down, and brown also. Turn them, add the tomato paste and stock and bring to a boil. Put back the onions, cover pan and simmer 30–40 minutes or until chicken is tender.

Taste for seasoning, chill and freeze in the casserole. Remove from casserole, wrap tightly and store in the freezer.

To serve: replace in casserole and thaw. Reheat, covered, on top of stove or in moderate oven (350°F) for 15–20 minutes or until bubbling. Serve with pilaf.

Bangkok Chicken

2 frying chickens (2½–3 lb each)
1 onion, sliced
1 carrot, quartered
bouquet garni
salt
6 peppercorns

For spiced butter
½ cup butter
½ teaspoon ground ginger
¼ teaspoon turmeric
pinch of cayenne
¼ cup mango chutney, finely
   chopped
juice of ½ lemon
1–2 cloves of garlic, crushed
bunch of watercress (for
   garnish)

Method

In a kettle put the whole chickens with the onion, carrot, bouquet garni, salt, peppercorns and water to cover. Add lid, bring to a boil and poach for 40 minutes or until chickens are tender; cool them in the liquid.

To make spiced butter: melt 2 tablespoons of the butter in a saucepan, add spices, cook gently for 2–3 minutes and cool. Cream the remaining butter and work in the spice mixture with the chutney, lemon juice, garlic and ½ teaspoon salt.

Drain the chickens, split them, discarding backbone, and spread the skin side with spiced butter. Chill them until the butter is firm, then wrap them tightly and freeze.

To serve: thaw and broil chickens, skin side up, until the skin is browned. Arrange on a platter, garnish with watercress and serve hot with broiled tomatoes and pilaf or cold with a rice salad.

Chicken and Tongue Rolls

1 cup (½ lb) cooked chicken,
   cut in strips
1 cup (½ lb) cooked tongue,
   cut in strips
4–6 tablespoons mayonnaise
8 thin slices of cooked ham
puff pastry (made with 1½ cups
   flour, ¾ cup butter, salt,
   ½ teaspoon lemon juice,
   6–8 tablespoons ice water)
1 egg, beaten to mix (for glaze)

One package ready-prepared flaky croissant dough can be substituted for puff pastry – unwrap it and roll in one piece as for puff pastry.

Method

Make the puff pastry dough and chill.

Mix the chicken and tongue with the mayonnaise, spread the mixture on the slices of ham and roll up. Roll the pastry dough about ¼ inch thick and cut into eight 3–3½ inch squares. Place a roll of ham on each, brush along one edge with water, fold dough around the ham and seal, leaving both ends open.

Roll out the dough trimmings and cut into narrow strips. Brush the rolls lightly with water and lay the strips over them to decorate. Wrap tightly and freeze.

To serve: thaw the rolls, set them on a baking sheet and brush with beaten egg to glaze. Bake in a hot oven (425°F) for 15–20 minutes or until puffed and brown. Serve hot or cold.

Pork Chops with Tomato Sauce

8 medium pork loin chops
2 tablespoons olive oil
¼ cup Marsala or sherry
bouquet garni

For tomato sauce
3 large tomatoes, seeded and
   coarsely chopped or 2 cups
   canned tomatoes, crushed
1 onion, chopped
2 tablespoons butter
1 bay leaf
½ teaspoon basil or thyme
2 cloves of garlic, crushed
salt and pepper
1 cup stock
kneaded butter, made with
   1 tablespoon butter and
   ½ tablespoon flour
¼ cup sour cream (for serving)
   – optional

Method

To make the sauce: sauté onion in the butter until soft, then add the tomatoes, herbs, garlic and seasoning. Cover and simmer until the tomatoes are pulpy. Add the stock and simmer, uncovered, for 15–20 minutes.

Work the sauce through a strainer, bring it back to a boil and simmer 5–10 minutes or until the flavor is concentrated. If necessary, whisk in the kneaded butter a little at a time to thicken it.

In a skillet heat the olive oil and slowly brown the pork chops on both sides. Add the Marsala or sherry with the bouquet garni, cover tightly and simmer 25–30 minutes or until the chops are tender.

Remove the chops and arrange them in a foil-lined baking dish. Strain the meat juices into the tomato sauce, season to taste and spoon the sauce over the chops. Chill.

Freeze, remove chops and sauce from the baking dish and wrap them tightly; store

the chops in the freezer.

To serve: replace chops and sauce in the baking dish and thaw. Reheat them, covered, in a moderate oven (350°F) for 15–20 minutes or until very hot and, if you like, spoon over sour cream before serving. Serve with pasta shells, tossed in butter or heavy cream.

Veal Sauté with Cheese

4–8 veal escalopes or 4 veal
   chops (about 1½ lb)
3 tablespoons butter
salt and pepper
½ cup white wine, or veal or
   chicken stock
4 slices of Gruyère or Bel Paese
   cheese

For mustard cream sauce
1 teaspoon Dijon-style mustard
2 tablespoons butter
1½ tablespoons flour
1 cup milk
¼ cup light cream

Method

In a skillet melt butter and sauté escalopes or chops over fairly low heat until golden on both sides, allowing 7–10 minutes for escalopes and 15–20 minutes for chops. Season, pour on wine or stock and simmer until most of the liquid has evaporated. Arrange escalopes or chops in a shallow foil-lined baking dish and set cheese slices on top of meat.

Make the sauce as for white sauce, stir in the mustard and season to taste. Spoon sauce over the veal, chill and then freeze it.

Remove meat from dish, wrap tightly and store in freezer.

To serve: replace meat and sauce in baking dish and thaw.

Bake in a moderate oven (350°F) for 20 minutes or until bubbling, and brown under broiler just before serving. Serve with freshly sautéed cucumber.

Veal Sauté Chasseur

$1\frac{1}{2}$–2 lb veal round or rump, cut in $1\frac{1}{2}$ inch cubes
1 cup ($\frac{1}{4}$ lb) mushrooms, sliced
2 tablespoons oil
2 tablespoons butter
4 shallots, finely chopped
1 tablespoon flour
1 cup white wine
$1\frac{1}{2}$ cups stock
2 teaspoons tomato paste
bouquet garni
salt and pepper

To garnish
1 tablespoon chopped fresh chervil or parsley
2–3 slices of bread, crusts removed, cut in triangles and fried in 3–4 tablespoons oil and butter, mixed (for croûtes)

Method
Heat the oil in a heavy flame-proof casserole, add the butter and when melted brown the veal on all sides, a few pieces at a time. Take the meat from the pan and keep warm.
Watchpoint: do not move or turn veal until it has had time to brown thoroughly on one side.
Lower the heat, add the mushrooms and sauté them for 1–2 minutes or until soft. Discard excess fat from the casserole, add shallots and stir in flour. Cook, stirring occasionally, until flour is a deep brown, then stir in wine and stock and bring to a boil. Add the tomato paste and bouquet garni, replace veal and season.

Cover casserole and bake in a moderate oven (350°F) for $1\frac{1}{4}$–$1\frac{1}{2}$ hours or until the veal is very tender. Remove the bouquet garni, taste for seasoning and chill. Remove veal from the casserole, wrap tightly and store in the freezer.
To serve: unwrap veal, replace in casserole and thaw. Reheat, covered, on top of stove or in a moderate oven (350°F) for 15–20 minutes or until bubbling. Sprinkle with chervil or parsley and arrange croûtes around the edge before serving. Buttered noodles or pilaf are good accompaniments.

Steak Roulades with Celery Stuffing

2 lb flank steak
2 tablespoons seasoned flour, made with pinch of salt and pinch of pepper
2 tablespoons oil
2 onions, diced
2 carrots, diced
1 cup white wine
1 cup stock
bouquet garni
kneaded butter made with 2 tablespoons butter, 1 tablespoon flour – optional
salt and pepper
$\frac{1}{4}$ cup heavy cream (to finish)

For celery stuffing
2 tablespoons butter
1 cup chopped celery
1 tablespoon chopped fresh fennel or 1 teaspoon fennel seed
1 clove of garlic, crushed
1 cup fresh white breadcrumbs
1 egg, beaten to mix

Method
Cut the steak diagonally in the largest possible $\frac{1}{4}$ inch slices.
To make celery stuffing:

heat the butter, add the celery, cover and cook gently for 15 minutes or until soft. Stir in the fennel or fennel seed, garlic and breadcrumbs, season well and add enough beaten egg to bind the mixture. Spread a little of the stuffing on each slice of the steak, roll up and tie with fine string. Coat roulades with the seasoned flour.
In a flameproof casserole, heat the oil and brown the roulades on all sides. Remove them, add the onion and carrot, lower the heat, cover and cook gently for 5–7 minutes. Place the beef roulades on top, add the white wine, stock and bouquet garni, cover the pan and braise in a moderate oven (350°F) for 1–$1\frac{1}{2}$ hours or until the roulades are very tender. Cool them slightly, lift out, remove the strings and set them in a baking dish lined with foil.
Strain the meat juices into a saucepan, bring to a boil and whisk in the kneaded butter, a little at a time. Simmer sauce for 2 minutes, taste for seasoning and spoon over the roulades. Chill.
Freeze them. Remove from the baking dish, wrap tightly and store in the freezer.
To serve: replace steak roulades in the baking dish and thaw. Reheat, covered, on top of the stove or in a moderate oven (350°F) for 20–25 minutes or until very hot. Stir in the cream and serve with braised Belgian endive.

Ragoût of Lamb

$1\frac{1}{2}$–2 lb shoulder of lamb, cut in 2 inch cubes
2 tablespoons oil
1 onion, chopped
1 tablespoon flour
1 tablespoon tomato paste
$\frac{3}{4}$ cup white wine
1–$1\frac{1}{2}$ cups stock
2 cloves of garlic, crushed
2 shallots, finely chopped
bouquet garni
salt and pepper
2 cups ($\frac{1}{2}$ lb) mushrooms, halved
2 tablespoons butter

Method
In a flameproof casserole heat the oil and fry the cubes of lamb over medium heat, a few pieces at a time, until they are browned on all sides. Take them out, add the onion and brown also. Stir in the flour and cook $\frac{1}{2}$ minute. Stir in the tomato paste, pour in the wine and stock and bring to a boil. Add the garlic, shallots, bouquet garni and seasoning and put back the cubes of lamb. Cover the pot and simmer on top of the stove or cook in a moderately low oven (325°F) for $1\frac{1}{2}$ hours or until the meat is tender.
Sauté the mushrooms in the butter and add to the lamb when it is cooked. Taste the ragoût for seasoning, chill and freeze in the casserole. Remove ragoût from the casserole, wrap it tightly and store in the freezer.
To serve: replace the ragoût in the casserole and thaw. Reheat, covered, on top of the stove or in a moderate oven (350°F) for 15–20 minutes or until bubbling. Serve with pilaf or kasha (see Volume 4).

Carbonade of beef is baked in the oven with ale or beer. It freezes well and is quick to reheat

Carbonade of Beef

1½–2 lb chuck or round steak, cut in 2 inch cubes
1 tablespoon beef drippings or oil
2 large onions, sliced
1 tablespoon flour
1 clove of garlic, crushed
1 cup hot water
1½ cups ale or beer
bouquet garni
pinch of ground nutmeg
pinch of sugar
1 teaspoon wine vinegar
salt and pepper

Method

In a flameproof casserole heat the drippings or oil and brown the meat on all sides a few pieces at a time. Remove the meat, add the onion, turn down the heat and cook slowly until well browned. Stir in the flour and garlic and pour in the water and ale or beer.

Replace the meat, add the bouquet garni, nutmeg, sugar, vinegar and seasoning and bring to a boil. Stir well to mix, cover tightly and bake in a moderately low oven (325°F) for 1½–2 hours or until the meat is very tender. Remove the bouquet garni, taste for seasoning and chill.

Freeze the carbonade, then remove it from the casserole, wrap tightly and store in the freezer.

To serve: replace the carbonade in the casserole and thaw it. Reheat, covered, on top of the stove or in a moderate oven (350°F) for 15–20 minutes or until bubbling. Serve with boiled potatoes and braised red cabbage.

Carbonade used to refer to any dish that was simmered for a long time over coals (charbon) but it has come to be associated mainly with this rich beef stew made with ale or beer — a typically Flemish dish.

Crêpes Farcies au Chou (Stuffed Cabbage Crêpes)

crêpe batter (made with 1½ cups milk, 1 cup flour, pinch of salt, 1 egg, 1 egg yolk, 1 tablespoon melted butter or oil)
little oil (for frying)
mornay sauce (made with 2 tablespoons butter, 2 tablespoons flour, 1½ cups milk, salt and pepper, pinch of dry mustard, 6 tablespoons grated Parmesan or dry Cheddar cheese)
2 tablespoons grated Parmesan or dry Cheddar cheese (for sprinkling)

For filling
1 small (about 1½ lb) green cabbage, shredded
2 tablespoons butter
1 onion, sliced
¼ lb piece bacon, cut in cubes and blanched
¼ cup stock
salt and pepper

Makes about 18 crêpes.

Method

Make the crêpe batter and let stand for 30 minutes. Fry the crêpes in the hot oil.

To make the filling: in a heavy flameproof casserole, heat the butter, add the onion and cook, covered, until soft. Add the blanched bacon cubes and continue cooking until golden brown. Stir in the shredded cabbage with the stock and seasoning and cover with buttered foil and a lid. Cook gently on top of the stove or bake in a moderate oven (350°F) for 40 minutes or until the cabbage is tender, stirring occasionally.

Make the mornay sauce.

Place a spoonful of cabbage filling on each crêpe, fold them in three and arrange, overlapping, in a foil-lined baking dish. Coat them with the mornay sauce and sprinkle with the cheese. Chill.

Freeze the stuffed crêpes. Take from the baking dish, wrap tightly and store in the freezer.

To serve: butter the baking dish, put in the crêpes and thaw. Reheat in a moderate oven (350°F) for 15–20 minutes or until the crêpes are bubbling and browned.

Chestnut parfait is decorated with rosettes of whipped cream and topped with candied orange peel

Chestnut Parfait

1 can (1 lb) sweetened
    chestnut purée
thick custard (made with
    1 cup milk, 2 tablespoons
    sugar, ½ vanilla bean or
    ½ teaspoon vanilla extract
    and 4 egg yolks)
1½ cups heavy cream, whipped
    until it holds a soft shape
3–4 tablespoons maraschino
    liqueur
½ cup crumbled marrons glacés
    (candied chestnuts) –
    optional
6–8 sticks of candied orange
    peel, cut in pieces

*4 parfait or stemmed wine
    glasses, or metal mold
    (5–6 cup capacity); pastry
    bag and star tube*

Candied orange peel is available at some candy counters or you can make it as described in tangerine sherbet.

Method
Make the custard and chill it. When cold, fold in 1 cup of the whipped cream with the maraschino liqueur. Beat ¾–1 cup of the remaining whipped cream into the chestnut purée to soften it.

To arrange in glasses: fill the chestnut purée and maraschino custard mixtures into the parfait or stemmed wine glasses in layers with the crumbled marrons glacés (if used), ending with chestnut purée.

Whip remaining cream until it holds a stiff peak, fill into pastry bag fitted with the star tube and pipe rosettes on top of parfait. Freeze until firm, then cover without pressing down on the cream, and store in the freezer.

Transfer parfaits to refrigerator 30 minutes before serving and sprinkle them with pieces of candied peel.

To arrange in a mold: spread chestnut purée mixture around the outside of the mold and sprinkle it with the marrons glacés (if used). Fill the center with the maraschino custard mixture, cover and freeze.

Unmold parfait by dipping it quickly in cold water and running a knife around the edge. Turn out onto a platter, decorate the outside with rosettes of whipped cream and top them with candied orange peel.

Tangerine Sherbet

6 tangerines
1 cup sugar
2 cups water
juice of 1 lemon
1 envelope gelatin
1 egg white
granulated sugar (for rolling)

Makes about 1½ quarts.

Method
Remove the peel from 2 tangerines in sections and reserve. Work the flesh through a strainer to obtain the juice. Squeeze juice from remaining tangerines and measure it – there should be about 1½ cups.

Dissolve half the sugar in 1 cup water, bring to a boil and simmer 5 minutes. Take from heat and stir into tangerine juice.

Add enough water to the lemon juice in a small pan to make ¼ cup, sprinkle over the gelatin and let stand 5 minutes or until spongy; dissolve over a pan of hot water and stir into the tangerine mixture. Chill, then pour into a shallow bowl or ice cube trays and freeze 1–2 hours or until slushy.

Whip the egg white until it holds a stiff peak. Take out the partly frozen tangerine mixture and beat well with a chilled beater in a chilled bowl. Add the egg white, cover tightly with foil and freeze 2–3 hours longer until firm. Beat it once more during freezing to prevent ice crystals from forming.

To store: transfer to a sealed container and keep in freezer.

Boil the reserved tangerine peel in lightly salted water for 15 minutes. Drain and cut into julienne strips. In a saucepan dissolve the remaining sugar in 1 cup water and bring to a boil. Add the tangerine peel and simmer very gently for 15–20 minutes or until the peel is almost transparent. Transfer to a strainer or rack to drain, then roll peel in granulated sugar and let stand 4–6 hours in a dry atmosphere to harden.

To serve: if sherbet is ready more than 2–3 hours before needed, transfer it to the refrigerator for 15–30 minutes before serving to soften slightly. Pile it in chilled sherbet glasses and top with candied tangerine peel.

Peppermint Ice Cream

2 eggs
2 egg yolks
⅓ cup sugar
2½ cups milk
peppermint flavoring (to taste)
1 cup heavy cream, whipped
    until it holds a soft shape
few drops of red food coloring

Makes about 1 quart.

Method
Beat eggs with egg yolks until mixed and whisk in sugar until mixture is smooth without starting to thicken. Scald milk and pour into egg mixture, stirring vigorously. Cool, then strain custard and add peppermint flavoring to taste.

Stir whipped cream into the custard and taste for flavor; add more peppermint, if necessary, and color it pink with red food coloring. Chill, then freeze in ice trays until slushy.

Take out the partly frozen ice cream and beat well with a chilled beater in a chilled bowl. Return to freezer and freeze 2–3 hours or until firm. If mixture is slow to freeze, beat once more to prevent ice crystals from forming.

To store: transfer to a sealed container or pack in a mold and seal tightly.

To serve: unmold ice cream onto a platter or shape into balls with an ice cream scoop.

Pears 'en Douillon'
(Pears in a Sleeve)

4 large ripe dessert pears
puff pastry (made with 1½ cups
　flour, ¾ cup butter, salt,
　½ teaspoon lemon juice,
　6–8 tablespoons ice water)
sugar syrup (made with 1 cup
　water and ½ cup sugar)
2 tablespoons raisins
2 tablespoons brandy

To finish
1 egg, beaten to mix (for glaze)
6 tablespoons red currant jelly
piece of angelica, cut in 4 strips
　(for decoration) – optional
½ cup heavy cream, stiffly
　whipped (for serving)

Method
Make the pastry dough and chill it.

Pare the pears, remove the stalks and carefully scoop out the cores with a teaspoon; do not cut right through the pears.

Make the sugar syrup, lower the pears into it so they are completely covered. Simmer 15–20 minutes or until pears are just tender; let cool in the syrup, then drain thoroughly.

Fill holes in the pears with the raisins mixed with the brandy.

Roll out dough fairly thinly, trim the edges and cut 4 squares large enough to enclose the pears. Turn each square of dough over and set a pear upright in the middle. Cut diagonally out to each corner of the dough and wrap it overlapping around the pear, keeping it upright and leaving a hole at the top. Roll out the dough trimmings and cut out stars or shapes with a small fancy cutter.

Brush the dough-wrapped pears with beaten egg and overlap the small shapes on them to hide the seams in the dough. Chill pears, wrap them tightly and freeze.

To serve: set oven at hot (425°F). Thaw pears and brush with beaten egg. Bake in the heated oven for 15–20 minutes or until the pastry is brown.

Melt the red currant jelly; pour a little warm jelly into the top of each pear and spear with a piece of angelica in the top, if you like, to resemble a stalk. Serve the pears hot with a separate bowl of whipped cream.

Set the pears upright when wrapping in pastry to prevent the brandy from running out

Cover the dough seams of the pears with stars cut from pastry trimmings

Strawberry Charlotte

1 pint fresh strawberries,
　hulled
3 eggs
2 egg yolks
¾ cup sugar
juice of ½ lemon
1 envelope gelatin
1 cup heavy cream, whipped
　until it holds a soft shape

To finish
¾ cup heavy cream, whipped
　until it holds a soft shape
1 package cats' tongue cookies
　or ladyfingers

*Charlotte mold (2 quart
　capacity); pastry bag and
　star tube*

Method
Lightly oil the mold.

Purée the strawberries in a blender or work them through a sieve – there should be 1 cup purée.

Put the eggs, egg yolks and sugar in a bowl and beat until mixed. Set the bowl over a pan of hot but not boiling water and beat until the mixture is thick and light and leaves a ribbon trail on itself when the beater is lifted. Take from the heat and beat until cool. If using an electric beater, no heat is needed.

Add enough water to the lemon juice to make ¼ cup, sprinkle the gelatin on top and let stand 5 minutes or until spongy. Melt over a pan of hot water and stir into the egg mixture with the strawberry purée. Chill over a pan of ice water, stirring, until it starts to thicken. Fold in the lightly whipped cream and pour at once into the prepared mold.

Cover and freeze until solid. Turn out of mold, wrap tightly and store in the freezer.

To serve: remove from the freezer to refrigerator to thaw 1–1½ hours before serving. Set on a platter, spread the sides with some of the lightly whipped cream and arrange the cats' tongues or ladyfingers overlapping around the sides.

Stiffly whip the remaining cream, fill into the pastry bag fitted with the star tube and pipe rosettes around the top of the charlotte.

The finished pear 'en douillon' – in a pastry sleeve – is served hot with whipped cream

Austrian rum cake is soaked in sweetened coffee-flavored rum, then decorated with cream and nuts

Austrian Rum Cake

1¼ cups self-rising flour
pinch of salt
¾ cup butter
¾ cup sugar
3 eggs, beaten to mix
1 cup strong black coffee
2 tablespoons sugar
  (or to taste)
3–4 tablespoons rum
2 cups Chantilly cream (made
  with 1 cup heavy cream,
  2–3 tablespoons sugar,
  1 teaspoon vanilla)
1 tablespoon flaked almonds,
  browned

*Ring mold or 8 inch springform
pan (2 quart capacity);
pastry bags and star tube*

Method
Set the oven at moderately hot (375°F). Grease the mold or pan and sift flour with the salt.

Cream the butter, gradually add the sugar and beat until light and soft. Beat in the eggs, a little at a time, then fold in the flour.

Pour the mixture into prepared mold and bake in the heated oven for about 25 minutes if using a ring mold or 35–40 minutes if using a springform pan. Cake should spring back when lightly pressed with a fingertip. Turn out onto a wire rack to cool. When cold, wrap tightly and freeze.

To serve: replace the cake in the mold and let thaw. Heat the coffee almost to boiling point, sweeten with the sugar to taste and flavor it with the rum. Spoon the hot coffee over the cake in the mold and let soak until all the liquid is absorbed.

Turn cake onto a platter and coat completely with Chantilly cream. Fill the remaining cream into the pastry bag fitted with the star tube and decorate the cake with rosettes of whipped cream. Top the rosettes with browned almonds and serve.

Fruit in Strawberry Cream

6–8 ripe pears, pared, cored
  and sliced, or peaches,
  peeled, pitted and sliced,
  or 1 quart fresh strawberries,
  raspberries or blueberries
¾ cup frozen sweetened
  strawberry purée, thawed
¾ cup heavy cream
candied violets (for decoration)

4 sherbet or stemmed glasses

This is a good way of using home-frozen strawberry purée. You can use any tart fruit for the purée, such as raspberries or cooked cranberries.

Method
Whip the cream until it begins to thicken, then beat in the thawed strawberry purée a little at a time and continue beating until the cream holds a soft shape.

Prepare the fruit, pile it in the glasses and at once spoon over the strawberry cream. Decorate with candied violets and chill before serving.

To Freeze Fruit Purée

Work fruit through a nylon strainer or purée it in a blender and strain to remove the seeds (if there are any). Beat in sugar to taste and pack in an airtight container, leaving a little space at the top for expansion.

Strawberries, raspberries, blackberries and blueberries can all be frozen in this way. When thawed, the purées are excellent for making sauces, mousses, soufflés and fruit fools.

Refrigerator Rolls

2 medium potatoes
4 cups flour
1 teaspoon salt
¼ cup butter
1 package dry or 1 cake
  compressed yeast
¾ cup lukewarm milk
2 teaspoons sugar
1 egg, beaten to mix
1 large egg, beaten with
  ½ teaspoon salt (for glaze)

The potatoes in this recipe make these rolls especially light. The dough keeps well for up to 1 week in the refrigerator if it is tightly covered or it can be frozen for up to 2 weeks. Makes 30–35 rolls.

Method
Cook the potatoes in their skins in boiling water for 15 minutes or until very tender. Drain and peel them while still hot and mash well or push them through a potato ricer into a large warm bowl.

Sift in the flour with the salt and rub in the butter with the fingertips until the mixture resembles crumbs; make a well in the center.

Sprinkle or crumble yeast over ½ cup of the lukewarm milk and let stand 5 minutes until dissolved. Stir in the remaining milk with the sugar, and pour into the well in the flour along with the beaten egg; work with the hand to form a dough. Turn onto a lightly floured board and knead until the mixture is smooth and elastic. Put dough in a greased bowl, cover and let rise in a warm place for 1–1½ hours or until doubled in bulk.

Work it to knock out the air, divide into 30–35 even-sized pieces and shape into rolls.

To refrigerate or freeze: cover the unbaked rolls tightly and store in refrigerator for up to 1 week or in freezer for up to 2 weeks.

To bake: let rolls thaw (if you have frozen them) and rise in a warm place until almost doubled in bulk — length of time depends on the original temperature of the dough. Set oven at hot (425°F).

When risen, brush the rolls with egg glaze and bake on greased baking sheets in the heated oven for 15 minutes or until browned.

Spiced pork tenderloin is sprinkled with parsley and served with fried rice (recipe is on page 44)

This week's menu is both easy and unusual. Eggs are arranged on a colorful corn and pimiento salad and enclosed in a layer of ham-enhanced aspic. Pork tenderloin in a spicy sauce is served with fried rice, and for dessert, fruits in any combination you choose are layered only with sugar to draw out the juices.

A wine that can echo the sweetness of pork in an orientally-inspired sauce, yet maintain the dryness that most Westerners prefer, would seem a tall order. But France and California provide suitable candidates in the whites which they make from the chenin blanc grape. From the Loire Valley district of Anjou comes a fruity, but crisp-tasting wine called Savennières. Its American counterpart is the varietal Chenin Blanc that is at its best when produced by a fine Napa Valley vineyard.

SPICE PORK FOR A CHANGE

Eggs Maryland

Spiced Pork Tenderloin

Fried Rice   *Green Salad*

Marinated Fruit Bowl

~~

*White wine – Savennières (Loire)
or Chenin Blanc (California)*

TIMETABLE

Day before
Wash greens for salad and store in plastic bag in refrigerator; make vinaigrette dressing.
Make aspic for eggs Maryland.

Morning
Prepare marinade for pork tenderloins; start marinating pork. Peel tomatoes, seed, slice and wrap in plastic wrap. Poach eggs; prepare corn mixture for eggs Maryland and chill. Arrange eggs on corn mixture, add ham to aspic and spoon over the dish; refrigerate. Cook rice for fried rice and keep covered.
Make marinated fruit bowl, cover and chill.

Assemble equipment for final cooking from 6:45 for dinner around 8:00 p.m.

Order of Work

6:45
Brown marinated pork pieces, add stock, cover and cook.
Make Chantilly cream for fruit bowl, if serving.

7:45
Fry the rice and keep warm. Transfer pork to serving dish; make sauce, spoon over pork and keep warm. Garnish eggs Maryland with small cress or watercress. Arrange salad greens in bowl, ready to toss with dressing.

8:00
Serve eggs Maryland.

You will find that **cooking times** given in the individual recipes for these dishes have sometimes been adapted in the timetable to help you when cooking and serving this menu as a party meal.

Appetizer

Eggs Maryland

8 eggs
1 can (11 oz) corn kernels drained, or 1 package frozen corn kernels cooked according to package directions and drained
6 thin slices of cooked ham, cut in julienne strips
1 slice of canned pimiento, drained and cut in strips
$\frac{1}{4}$ cup heavy cream, whipped until it holds a soft shape
salt and pepper
$\frac{1}{4}$ teaspoon paprika (or to taste)
juice of $\frac{1}{2}$ lemon
2 cups cool but still liquid aspic (see right)
box of small cress or watercress (for garnish)

Method
Poach the eggs and keep them in a bowl of cold water until needed.

Mix corn, pimiento and cream together and season well with salt, pepper, paprika and lemon juice. Spoon the mixture onto a deep platter and chill.

Drain and dry the eggs on paper towels or on a dish towel, place them on top of the corn mixture and chill again.

In a bowl mix the ham strips and aspic; set over a pan of ice water and, when aspic is on the point of setting, spoon it over the eggs to coat them. Just before serving, garnish the dish with small cress or watercress.

Quick Aspic

1 can consommé
$\frac{1}{2}$ envelope gelatin
1–2 tablespoons brandy

Method
Sprinkle the gelatin over 3 tablespoons of the consommé in a small pan and let stand 5 minutes until spongy. Dissolve over gentle heat and stir into the remaining consommé with the brandy or sherry.

Drain poached eggs and arrange them on corn, pimiento and cream mixture

Serve eggs Maryland as an appetizer, garnished with small cress or watercress

Entrée

Spiced Pork Tenderloin

$1\frac{1}{2}$–2 lb pork tenderloin, cut in 2 inch pieces
$\frac{1}{4}$ cup butter
1 large onion, chopped
1 cup stock
3 tomatoes, peeled, seeded and sliced
1 tablespoon chopped parsley

For marinade
2 tablespoons soy sauce
1 tablespoon Worcestershire sauce
$\frac{1}{4}$ cup ketchup
1 tablespoon plum or apricot jam
1 tablespoon honey
1 teaspoon Dijon-style mustard
salt and pepper
$\frac{1}{2}$ teaspoon sugar (or to taste)
fried rice (for serving)

Method
Melt about $1\frac{1}{2}$ tablespoons of the butter in a deep flame-proof dish and stir in all ingredients for marinade. Take from heat, put in pork pieces, turning them over until they are well coated. Let stand in marinade for at least 30 minutes. Drain the pork pieces reserving the marinade.

In a frying pan heat remaining butter and add pork. Stir in the onion and fry slowly until pork is browned on all sides. Pour in the stock, cover and simmer for $\frac{3}{4}$–1 hour or until pork pieces are tender.

Transfer the pork pieces to a warm serving dish and pour the reserved marinade into the pan. Boil until it is reduced to $\frac{1}{4}$ cup, then add the sliced tomatoes. Cook 3–4 minutes longer and spoon sauce over the pork pieces. Sprinkle with chopped parsley and serve

with fried rice and a green salad.

For spiced pork, cook the tomato slices in marinade before spooning it over the pork pieces

Accompaniment to entrée

Fried Rice

$1\frac{1}{4}$ cups rice
2 tablespoons olive oil
1 small onion, chopped
salt and pepper
2 teaspoons soy sauce
2 eggs, beaten to mix

Method
Cook rice in boiling salted water for 12 minutes or until just tender. Drain, rinse with hot water and drain again thoroughly.

In a skillet heat the oil, add the onion and cook over low heat until soft but not browned. Stir rice into skillet and fry until it begins to brown, stirring occasionally. Stir in seasoning to taste and the soy sauce and eggs. Continue cooking, stirring constantly with a fork, for 5–7 minutes until the mixture looks dry. Serve rice at once.

Add the soy sauce and beaten eggs to the fried rice and continue stirring until it looks dry

Dessert

Marinated Fruit Bowl

For this dish choose at least 4 contrasting fruits to make about 5 cups of fruit in all.

To prepare the fruit: hull the strawberries and wash only if necessary; pick over blueberries or blackberries, and wash and drain them thoroughly; peel and slice bananas; wash, drain and seed grapes; peel and segment oranges and grapefruit (see box); pare, core and slice apples and pears; halve, pit, peel and slice peaches; cut melon into cubes or balls; wash, drain and pit cherries; peel, core and cut pineapple in chunks.

Layer the fruit in a glass bowl, sprinkling each layer with confectioners' or granulated sugar to taste — the amount needed depends on tartness of fruit. If you like, sprinkle 3–4 tablespoons brandy, rum or Cointreau on top.

Cover the bowl tightly and chill at least 6 hours so the sugar draws out fruit juices. If you like, serve with Chantilly cream made with 1 cup heavy cream, stiffly whipped and flavored with 1 tablespoon sugar and $\frac{1}{2}$ teaspoon vanilla.

To segment oranges and grapefruits: with a serrated-edge knife, cut the peel, white pith and skin from fruit, using a sawing motion. Cut down between membrane and flesh to loosen segments, folding back the membrane like the leaves of a book.

Marinated fruit bowl is a very colorful dessert

Slices of norimaki sushi (vinegared rice and fish in seaweed) are
arranged on bamboo leaves and served with sake (recipe is on page 50)

JAPANESE COOKING

Japanese food is as beguiling to the eye as it is pleasing to the palate. The preparation is a harmony of texture, form, color and flavor. Even the vessels in which the food is cooked and served conform to the method by which it is prepared.

There are Occidentals and, for that matter, other Orientals, who insist that Japanese cooking lacks flavor and is without variety; this is not so. The cooking of Japan is delicately flavored and so subtly varied that its nuances are not always recognized.

The Japanese insist that their cooking cannot be completely enjoyed unless it is eaten with chopsticks. That depends on how adept one is with them, but Japanese food is always prepared to be eaten with chopsticks. Before cooking it is cut up so it can be managed with the sticks; knives are not a part of Japanese tableware.

Meals follow the seasons in substance and the average family generally sits down to a breakfast of hearty soup, eggs or fish or seaweed in a soy-flavored sauce, and tea. At midday the family may partake of cooked fish, vegetables (plain or with a dressing) and tea. A typical dinner menu may provide a clear soup or one with a little bean curd or leek, cooked fish (generally fried) or a preparation with meat, and cooked and pickled vegetables, plus tea. The tea varies depending on the meal. At breakfast it is regular tea, a better quality at midday, and the best at dinner.

Although bread is now seen on the tables of Japan, rice is a staple at all meals. Dessert, if any, is likely to be fresh fruit or, on special occasions, a sweet soup or a cake made of sweet potato paste and cooked fruit.

Japanese cooking is said to require lengthy preparation and this reputation is well founded. However, the actual cooking is quick, as you will discover with the recipes that follow.

Alvin Kerr, author of our feature on **Japanese cooking,** is a lecturer, demonstrator and author of many articles on all aspects of food. Educated in Europe, he has traveled extensively throughout Japan and has often demonstrated Japanese cooking. For many years a contributing editor to 'Gourmet' magazine, he is co-author of a new cookbook, 'The Family Cookbook: Italian' published by Holt, Rinehart and Winston.

Glossary

Aemono: cooked foods.
Ajinomoto: monosodium glutamate.
Daikon: white radish.
Dashi: clear soup.
Ginnan: ginkgo nuts.
Katsuobushi: dried bonito.
Kombu: dried kelp.
Mirin: mixture of wine and sake (rice wine).
Miso: paste of fermented soybean and malted wheat.
Misoshiru: basic soybean paste soup.
Mushimono: steamed dishes.
Nabemono: pan-cooked dishes.
Nori: edible seaweed.
Sake: rice wine.
Sashimi: fillets of raw fish eaten with various accompaniments. Whole menus may be composed of varied types of sashimi.
Shiitake: dried mushrooms.
Shirataki: noodles (vermicelli).
Shoyu: soy sauce.
Sudare: small bamboo mat.
Sushi: cooked fish rolled in seaweed.

Taro: Japanese root vegetable.
Tempura: pieces of fish, meat, poultry or vegetable dipped in batter and lightly fried. Includes at least 6 ingredients – often more – and must be served straight from the pan so they remain crisp.
    Serve with individual bowls of soy-flavored sauce for dipping and a plate of chopped seasoning like horseradish.
Tsukemono: various pickled vegetables.
Tufo: bean curd.
Wasabi: dried and powdered Japanese horseradish.

Japanese Ingredients

All of the ingredients required in the following recipes are available here in shops specializing in oriental foods.

Bean curd (tufo) is a square cake of compressed soybean. It is also available canned and in powdered form.
Bonito, dried (katsuobushi) is a kind of tuna fish available already flaked. It keeps very well and is primarily used as flavoring for dashi (the cooking liquid used for broths or in the preparation of fish, poultry and meat).
Ginger root is used extensively in Japanese cooking, usually freshly grated.
Ginkgo nuts (ginnan) are available fresh or canned. They combine well with chicken.
Kelp, dried (kombu) is a kind of seaweed dried in sheets. Cut in small pieces, it is a main ingredient of dashi.
Monosodium glutamate (ajinomoto) is used in small quantities to heighten the natural

flavor of a dish. It is available in containers and sold in markets as MSG or under various trade names. There have been warnings against the effect of MSG, but it has been used in the Orient for decades. Buy a good brand that is 99% pure.
Mushrooms, dried (shiitake) are packaged whole. They must be soaked in water and should be shredded or chopped before using.
Noodles (shirataki). These thread-like noodles are similar to vermicelli and come in cans or packages.
Radish, white (daikon) is a bland fresh root similar to a turnip.
Horseradish, dried and powdered (wasabi) is green in color and very hot. Mix to a paste with water and stand 3–5 minutes before using.
Sake (rice wine) is served as an accompaniment to Japanese meals. It is heated gently in the bottle before pouring into a tiny jug for serving. Sake is also used in cooking.
Mirin, a sweet blend of wine and sake, is used only for cooking. Sherry may be substituted in recipes.
Seaweed (nori) is one of several kinds of seaweed used in Japanese cooking. It comes dried in thin greenish-black sheets.
Snow peas, pea pods or sugar peas are flat pea pods usually 3–4 inches long and used whole or shredded after tips and strings have been removed by hand.
Soybean paste (miso) is a mixture of malted wheat and mashed cooked soybeans fermented for several months. It is used for flavoring, particularly of miso soup.
Taro is a root vegetable native to Jamaica, the Pacific Islands, Japan and central Asia. Generally the size of a Jerusalem artichoke, it can be as large as 5 lb.

Shoyu, the Japanese **soy sauce,** is considered to be richer and more highly flavored than the Chinese variety. Because it is matured, it seems less salty, although it may not actually contain less salt. It is a pungent brown liquid flavoring made principally from soybeans and roasted corn.

Soup Garnishes

The first three garnishes are shown in the photograph, right.

Lime: arrange 3 very thin slices of lime overlapping in a circle.
Mushroom: arrange very thin slices of mushroom with a few rings from the white part of a scallion on top.
Shrimps: interlock 2 shrimps so that 2 tails face out in opposite directions. Top with a small piece of fern.
Bamboo shoot fan: make very fine slices three-quarters of the way across a $1\frac{1}{2}$ inch slice of bamboo shoot. Press the base to flare the 'ribs' of the fan.
Flower petals: arrange a few petals of chrysanthemum or nasturtium blossoms on top of the soup.
Leaves: arrange shreds of the following – cabbage, spinach leaves, sweet red and green peppers, or white nasturtium leaves on top of the soup.
Lemon pine needles: cut very thin lemon rind into slivers to resemble pine needles (which in Japan represent longevity). Arrange in a random little clump to look as if they had fallen from a tree.

Omelet: cut paper-thin strands from a very thin omelet and arrange on top of soup (see shredded omelet on page 51).
Radish: cut a very thin slice from a red radish and pierce a tiny hole in the center with a skewer. Thread a tiny sprig of parsley through the hole so that the flower part sits on the radish round.
Root vegetables: cut very thin slices of white turnip, carrot, radish or other root vegetables and trim into flower shapes with an aspic or truffle cutter (see pages 56–57).

Dashi
(Broth)

6 cups water
1 inch square dried kelp
$\frac{1}{8}$ teaspoon monosodium glutamate
$\frac{1}{2}$ cup flaked dried bonito

Serve as broth, clear or with a garnish. Dashi is also the basis for heartier soups and is widely used as a cooking liquid for preparations of fish, poultry and meat.

Method
In a saucepan bring the water, kelp and monosodium glutamate almost to a boil – it should not actually bubble. Remove kelp. Add bonito and bring the water completely to a boil.
Remove the pan from the heat and leave until the bonito flakes sink to the bottom. Strain the clear liquid and use as required.

Misoshiru
(Soybean Paste Soup)

4 cups dashi, heated
$\frac{1}{3}$ cup soybean paste

Use as a basis for hearty soups or add cooked vegetables, fish, shellfish, chicken or pork, as you like.

Method
In a bowl blend 1 cup of the heated dashi into the bean paste. Stir the mixture into the remaining dashi.

Kakimiso
(Oyster Soup)

1 pint shucked oysters with their liquor
4 cups misoshiru
1–2 teaspoons cornstarch, mixed to a paste with 1–2 tablespoons cold water
dash of Tabasco

Method
In a saucepan combine the oysters with their liquor, the misoshiru and the cornstarch paste.
Simmer the soup for 2–3 minutes or until the oysters rise to the top and the liquid thickens. Season with Tabasco to taste.

Misoshiru (soybean paste soup) can be garnished with interlocked shrimps, slices of lime, or mushrooms with scallion rings

For norimaki sushi, layer the mushrooms and spinach on rice spread on sheets of seaweed

To complete the sushi, use the sudare (bamboo mat) as a guide and carefully roll up ingredients

Norimaki Sushi
(Vinegared Rice
and Fish in Seaweed)

1 cup quantity Japanese
   vinegared rice

For filling
6 fresh salmon fillets or
   steaks, each about 6 X 4
   inches and $\frac{1}{2}$ inch thick
18 large spinach leaves
6 dried mushrooms (about $\frac{1}{2}$ oz)
1 teaspoon soy sauce
1 teaspoon mirin or sherry
$\frac{1}{4}$ teaspoon sugar
2 cups water
1 tablespoon vinegar
$\frac{3}{4}$ teaspoon salt
1 scallion, white part only
3–4 celery leaves
3–4 coriander seeds
shredded omelet
$\frac{1}{2}$ teaspoon dried radish powder
6 sheets of seaweed, each
   about 8 X 6 inches

6 small bamboo mats (sudare),
* or sheets of heavy waxed*
* paper (for rolling) – optional*

This traditional Japanese preparation, one of a variety called **sushi**, combines specially cooked rice with fish, eggs and vegetables, rolled in tissue-thin sheets of seaweed called **nori**. Serves 6–8 people.

Method
Cook the vinegared rice and keep warm.

To make filling: trim and wash spinach leaves and blanch in lightly salted boiling water for 30 seconds or until just beginning to wilt. Drain and pat dry with paper towels.

Soften the mushrooms by soaking them in just enough water to cover for 15–20 minutes; remove and discard stems. Cook the mushrooms for 5 minutes in the soaking water with the soy sauce,

50

mirin or sherry and sugar. Drain the mushrooms and cut them into thin strips.

In a kettle simmer the water, vinegar, $\frac{1}{2}$ teaspoon of the salt, scallion, celery leaves and coriander seeds for 15 minutes. Add the salmon fillets or steaks and poach gently for about 1 minute or until they are no longer transparent in the center. Drain well.

Make the 'omelet'.

Moisten the radish powder with a few drops of cold water and work to a smooth paste. Slightly warm the sheets of seaweed on a baking sheet in a low oven (250°F) for 5–10 minutes.

To complete the dish, place 1 sheet of seaweed on a bamboo mat or wax paper, if using. Spread one-sixth of the rice evenly on the seaweed, leaving a 1 inch border on all sides. Sprinkle one-sixth of the mushroom strips over the rice and add 1 salmon fillet or steak (divided into pieces free of any bone). Dot this with one-sixth or less of the radish paste and arrange 3 blanched spinach leaves on top, overlapping slightly.

Watchpoint: the radish paste is very, very hot so be careful not to add more than is specified.

Cover spinach with one-sixth of the shredded omelet.

Using the mat or wax paper as a guide, carefully roll ingredients in the sheet of seaweed, keeping the filling centered and making the roll as tight as possible.

Arrange the rest of the filling in the same way on the remaining sheets of seaweed and roll them as above. Tie bamboo mat rolls with their attached strings, or tie wax paper rolls with string to hold them firmly.

Let the rolls mellow in refrigerator for 1 hour before untying them, removing bamboo mats or wax paper, if using, and cutting rolls into slices. Arrange the slices attractively on a platter lined with bamboo leaves, if you like. Serve as an hors d'œuvre or appetizer.

Japanese Vinegared Rice

1 cup small grain rice
1$\frac{1}{8}$ cups water
2 tablespoons vinegar
$\frac{1}{2}$ teaspoon salt
$\frac{1}{2}$ teaspoon sugar
pinch of monosodium glutamate

If using long grain rice, increase the water to 2 cups.

Method
For 1 cup quantity: thoroughly wash and drain the rice. Put it in a bowl, cover with a cloth and let stand for 2 hours. Cover with cold water and let soak 30 minutes; drain again.

Put rice in a saucepan with the water and bring to a boil over high heat. Reduce heat to medium and cook rice for 5 minutes. Reduce heat to low, cover, and continue cooking for 15 minutes longer. Turn off the heat and let the rice steam for 10 minutes.

In a bowl combine the vinegar, salt, sugar and monosodium glutamate. Transfer cooked rice to a warm bowl. Quickly stir in seasoned vinegar and, at the same time, fan the rice vigorously. This simultaneous stirring and fanning makes the rice glisten.

Shredded Omelet

For 2 egg quantity: beat the eggs with 1 teaspoon cold water and $\frac{1}{2}$ teaspoon mirin or sherry, $\frac{1}{4}$ teaspoon sugar and salt. In a large skillet (about 10 inches) heat 1 teaspoon peanut oil.

Add the eggs and swirl them around to cover the bottom of the pan evenly and thinly. Cook the eggs until they are just set, turn and cook them briefly on the other side.

Remove the 'omelet' to a cutting board, roll it into a cylinder and cut it crosswise into very thin strands. Separate the strands to prevent them from sticking.

Sashimi
(Sliced Raw Fish)

1$\frac{1}{2}$ lb piece of fresh fish (sea bass or tuna)
1 cup finely shredded lettuce
1 cup finely shredded Japanese or other bland white radish, or white turnip

For dipping sauce
1 cup Japanese soy sauce
1 teaspoon finely grated fresh ginger root
1 teaspoon wine vinegar

Method
Remove skin and bones from fish; cut it across the grain, at an angle of about 30 degrees, into slices about 1$\frac{1}{2}$ inches long and $\frac{1}{2}$ inch thick. (The fish can be cut neatly and easily if the knife blade is rubbed frequently with bland cooking oil.) Chill the fish thoroughly.

Arrange equal quantities of lettuce and radish or turnip in separate mounds on 4 individual serving plates, with equal portions of fish between mounds; overlap the slices slightly.

Combine soy sauce, ginger and vinegar, pour mixture into 4 small bowls; serve as a dipping sauce for fish and vegetables.

Torisashi
(Chicken Sashi)

1½ lb boned breasts of chicken
cut in thin slices, 2 inches
long
1 cucumber
½ cup finely shredded fresh
horseradish

For dipping sauce
1 cup Japanese soy sauce
1 teaspoon vinegar

Method

Remove skin from chicken
and place the slices in a deep-
fry basket or colander and
lower into a large kettle of
boiling water. Leave 30
seconds, raise basket or colander, let chicken drain and
immerse again for 30 sec-
onds longer. Drain well and
cool.

Peel the cucumber, cut it in
half lengthwise, scoop out the
seeds with a teaspoon and,
with a vegetable peeler, cut it
into paper-thin slices about
1½ inches long. Squeeze dry
between paper towels and
chill.

Arrange chicken, cucumber
and horseradish on 4 individual serving plates. Combine
the soy sauce and vinegar in
individual bowls for dipping
and serve with the sashi.

Chawan Mushi
(Chicken in Custard)

½ lb boned breasts of chicken,
thinly sliced
4 dried mushrooms (about ½ oz)
4 large eggs
2 cups dashi (see page 49)
2 tablespoons mirin or sherry
¼ teaspoon monosodium
glutamate
¼ cup Japanese soy sauce
6 cooked, peeled small shrimps
6 shelled ginkgo nuts, fresh
or canned
4 spinach leaves
4 lemon wedges (for garnish)

This is one of the most popular
of the mushimono (steamed
preparations).

Method

Soften the mushrooms by
soaking in just enough water to
cover for 15–20 minutes.
Drain, reserve liquid and rub
mushrooms between paper
towels to remove skins.

In a bowl beat eggs and
combine them with dashi,
mirin or sherry, monosodium
glutamate, 2 tablespoons soy
sauce and reserved mushroom
liquid.

In a bowl combine the
chicken pieces, shrimps,
sliced mushrooms and ginkgo
nuts and stir remaining soy
sauce into them.

Place equal portions of the
chicken mixture in 4 individual
serving bowls or cups (1½ cup
capacity each). Pour over equal
quantities of the egg mixture and float a spinach leaf
on each. Cover each bowl or
cup tightly with lightly oiled
foil and set in a water bath.
Cover and cook over low heat
for 12 minutes or until a knife
inserted comes out clean.
Watchpoint: do not overcook
or the custard may separate.

Remove foil coverings and
serve hot custard in bowls or
cups with a wedge of lemon.

Tempura

18 cooked, unpeeled shrimps
(about 1 lb)
½ lb thick halibut fillet
1 small eggplant (about ½ lb)
1 large green pepper
16 crisp fresh green beans
flour (for dredging)
peanut oil (for frying)
sesame oil (for frying)

For batter
1 cup flour
1 egg, lightly beaten
1 cup cool water

To serve
½ cup shredded Japanese or
other bland white radish, or
white turnip
¼ cup grated fresh ginger root
1 cup clam broth or clam juice
¼ cup Japanese soy sauce
¼ cup mirin or sherry

Fat thermometer

Method

Peel the shrimps, leaving tail
shells intact.

Cut the halibut into 1 inch
squares. Peel the eggplant
and cut it into 1½ inch lengths
about ½ inch thick. Split the
pepper, remove seeds and
membrane and cut the flesh
into 8 pieces of equal size.
Trim the green beans.

To make batter: lightly beat
the flour into the egg and
water to make a rather lumpy
batter. Dredge the shrimps,
halibut and vegetables with
more flour and dip them
into the batter. Drain excess.

Pour equal quantities of the
oils into a deep saucepan or
deep fat bath to a depth of
about 2 inches and heat to
350°F on a fat thermometer.
Fry the fish and vegetable
pieces a few at a time in the
hot oil for 3 minutes or until
they are golden.

Serve them piece by piece
as soon as they are done.

Serve each person a little
radish or turnip, grated ginger,
and a bowl of the combined
clam broth or juice, soy sauce
and mirin or sherry for dipping.

Spinach
with Sesame

1½ lb spinach, leaves only
¼ cup sesame seeds, toasted
¼ cup Japanese soy sauce

This recipe is among the
aemono (cooked foods),
usually vegetables, served
with a dressing.

Method

Wash the spinach leaves thoroughly and drain them by
shaking off the water. Cook
them in the water that still
clings to them for 2–3 minutes or until they wilt. Drain
and pat dry with paper towels.
Transfer the leaves to a bowl.

Crush the sesame seeds to
a powder between sheets of
wax paper or in a mortar and
pestle or work them in a
blender.

In a mortar and pestle, or in
a bowl, work the powdered
seeds and the soy sauce to a
thin paste with a wooden
spoon. Cut the drained
spinach into small pieces (do
not chop) and toss with the
prepared dressing; serve in
individual bowls.

Tempura includes fried halibut, eggplant, green beans, green pepper and large shrimps

Sukiyaki

1½ lb lean sirloin steak
4 dried mushrooms (about ½ oz)
¼ lb noodles (shirataki), dry or canned
2 tablespoons sake
1 cup dashi (see page 49)
¼ lb beef suet, cut in small cubes
2 tablespoons sugar
pinch of monosodium glutamate
½ cup Japanese soy sauce
8 scallions, cut into 1½ inch lengths
1 large Bermuda or sweet onion, thinly sliced
2 carrots, cut in diagonal slices
2 cups shredded Chinese cabbage
6 medium button mushrooms, sliced
¼ lb snow peas, trimmed
1 cup thinly sliced fresh bamboo shoots
½ lb spinach (leaves only)
8 cubes of bean curd (tufo) — each 1 inch
4 eggs, beaten to mix (optional)

This, the most famous of Japan's nabemono (pan-cooked dishes), is almost as popular here as it is in Japan. Sukiyaki is prepared at the table in an electric skillet or in a large heavy iron skillet on a portable stove, with all the ingredients attractively arranged on platters or trays.

Method

To prepare the ingredients: soften the dried mushrooms by soaking in just enough water to cover for 15–20 minutes. Drain, reserving the liquid, and cut them into thin slices.

If dry noodles are used, soak them in cold water for 1 hour. Drain, discarding liquid. If using canned ones, drain thoroughly.

Cut the steak into paper-thin slices about 3 inches long.

Heat the reserved mushroom liquid, sake and dashi together.

To cook the sukiyaki: fry the cubes of suet in a skillet over medium heat. When they have rendered about 3 tablespoons fat, remove and discard them. Add the slices of steak and cook them quickly for 15 seconds on each side. They should be underdone. Sprinkle them with the sugar and monosodium glutamate and pour over the hot sake and dashi mixture.

Continue cooking for 30 seconds longer and move the slices of steak to the side of the pan.

Put the scallions, onion, carrot slices and cabbage into the center of the pan and cook them, stirring constantly, for exactly 2 minutes. Move them to another side of the pan and place the mushrooms, snow peas, bamboo shoots, spinach, bean curd and noodles in the center. Cook them also for exactly 2 minutes.

Guests should serve themselves some of each group of ingredients as they are cooked, dipping them, if they like, into beaten egg served in small individual bowls.

More servings may be added and cooked as required.

Japanese Pickled Radish

1 lb Japanese or other bland white radish with leaves
2 tablespoons salt
1–2 teaspoons finely grated fresh ginger root or orange rind (optional)

For dressing
2 tablespoons Japanese soy sauce
2 tablespoons white wine vinegar

A main meal in Japan is considered incomplete without tsukemono (pickled vegetables), the Japanese version of salad. Cabbage cut into wedges, thinly sliced cucumber, turnip, carrots, or unpeeled eggplant cut into cubes may be combined and pickled in the same way as radish.

Method

Wash the radishes and leaves thoroughly. Trim off the leaves and chop them. Sprinkle them with 1 tablespoon salt and rub it in. Let the leaves stand for 2–3 minutes, then squeeze out any liquid.

Cut the radish into long, thin strips, combine with the leaves and sprinkle with the remaining salt. Transfer the radish and leaves to a small crock or bowl and place a wooden cover or plate directly on them. Place a 2 lb weight on top and let the mixture mellow for 4–5 hours. Then press out the accumulated liquid.

To make dressing: combine soy sauce and white wine vinegar and toss with the radish. If you like, sprinkle over a little finely grated ginger or orange rind.

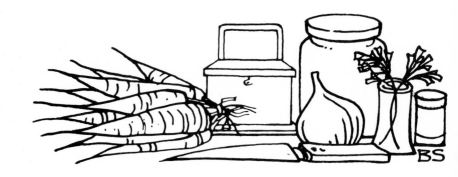

Raw ingredients for sukiyaki are arranged on platters: (left) thread-like noodles, button mushrooms, cubes of bean curd and snow peas; (below) paper-thin steaks; (right) spinach leaves, sliced carrots and onions, shredded cabbage, bamboo shoots, scallions and dried mushrooms.

Vegetable garnishes include: white radish, sliced; carrots neatly cut into julienne strips, scalloped circles, oak leaves and diagonal boat shapes; chrysanthemum turnips — a half cut and finished one; and scallion fans or brushes

Preparation of Vegetables

Cutting and slicing vegetables is an art and an essential part of Japanese cooking. There are endless variations to the shapes that can be made from different vegetables. Firm, carefully cut vegetables can even be made into delicately carved snowflakes.

Daikon (white radish) can be cut into the thinnest possible slices, then made into squares, semi-circles, miniature squares, or even cut so thinly from a round that it is nearly transparent.

Carrots can be cut into very fine julienne strips, scalloped and shaped into circles. A carrot can be made into a boat shape or trimmed to nearly a quarter of its original size and reshaped, with stem trimmed and left on.

Scallions can be made into fans or brushes. Trim off the end and leave 3 inches of the lighter part; cut one-sixteenth inch slices threequarters of the way down and soak in ice water to curl the fine ends.

Chrysanthemum Turnips

4 medium white turnips, peeled
1 teaspoon salt
$\frac{1}{4}$ cup white wine vinegar
2 tablespoons mirin or sherry
1 tablespoon sugar
2 teaspoons finely chopped sweet red pepper

Chrysanthemum turnips, another pickled vegetable, are usually an accompaniment to broiled fish. They are a popular festival preparation.

Method
Place 2 chopsticks horizontally in front of you on a chopping board and place 1 turnip between them, root down. With a very sharp thin knife make vertical cuts, about one-sixteenth inch apart over entire top, down through the turnip to the chopsticks. The sticks will prevent you from cutting entirely through the turnip.

Give the turnip a quarter turn, clockwise, so the cuts run from left to right. Cut down, as before, across these first cuts. Then cut the other 3 turnips in the same way.

Sprinkle the cut tops of the turnips with the salt and let stand for about 30 minutes. Rinse in cool water and drain.

Arrange them on a platter. Combine the vinegar, mirin or sherry and sugar and spoon over the turnips. Sprinkle $\frac{1}{2}$ teaspoon of the chopped pepper in the center of each turnip and serve.

Hikichamanju (Bean Paste Bun)

2 cups flour
1$\frac{1}{2}$ teaspoons baking powder
1 teaspoon powdered green tea
$\frac{2}{3}$ cup sugar
$\frac{2}{3}$ cup water
1$\frac{1}{3}$ cup bean paste, sieved

This is one of the Japanese desserts served on special occasions. Makes about 12 buns.

Method
Sift flour with the baking powder and the powdered tea into a bowl. Dissolve the sugar in the water and stir the liquid, a little at a time, into the flour mixture to make a firm dough.

Divide dough into 12 equal portions and roll each with your hands into a ball. Make a hole in each ball, fill it with 2 tablespoons bean paste and enclose it completely.

Arrange balls on a baking sheet. Spread a very wet dish towel on the bottom of a steamer. Set the baking sheet on a rack over it, cover and steam the buns over moderately high heat for 15 minutes. Serve at room temperature.

GIRLS' FESTIVAL

Each year March 3 heralds the beginning of the Girls' Festival in Japan, a three-day celebration when the girls display their doll collections and entertain friends with foods prepared especially for the young. The recipes following are served on this occasion.

Onigari-yaki (Broiled Shrimps in Soy Sauce)

24 cooked, peeled large shrimps (about 1$\frac{1}{2}$ lb)
$\frac{1}{3}$ cup mirin or sherry
$\frac{1}{2}$ cup Japanese soy sauce
2 tablespoons sugar

8 kebab or bamboo skewers

Method
In a saucepan over moderate heat boil mirin or sherry and soy sauce with sugar for 2 minutes or until the liquid is reduced by about one-quarter. Cool the mixture, then immerse the shrimps in it and leave for 1–2 minutes. Remove them and thread 3 on each of the skewers.

Broil the shrimps for 3 minutes over a moderately hot charcoal fire or 4–5 inches from the broiler, brushing them with the sauce and turning them after each minute.

Serve hot, 2 skewers for a serving.

'Shellfish' Sushi

½ cup quantity Japanese
   vinegared rice (see page 51)
3 dried mushrooms (about ⅓ oz)
4 eggs
2 tablespoons Japanese soy
   sauce
2 tablespoons sugar
½ teaspoon salt
1 tablespoon dashi (see
   page 49)

5–6 inch skillet

This recipe contains no fish
but takes its name from the
shell shape of the finished
'omelets'.

Method
Cook the rice and keep warm.

Soften the mushrooms by
soaking them in water to
cover for 15–20 minutes,
drain and cut into thin slices.

Combine mushrooms with
the cooked rice and season
the mixture with the soy sauce
and 1 tablespoon of the sugar.

In a bowl beat the eggs
with the salt, dashi and
remaining sugar. Brush the
skillet lightly with oil and
heat it. Pour in 3 tablespoons
of the egg mixture and swirl
it around to coat the bottom of
the pan thinly and evenly.
Cook the 'omelet' over
medium heat for 30 seconds
or until the egg is just set.

Turn the omelet carefully
and cook it quickly on other
side. Keep warm. Continue to
make 8 omelets with remaining egg mixture. Fold each in
half and in half again to make
a cone.

Heat a metal skewer and
sear one side of each omelet
with 3 lines fanning out along
the cone to the open end. Fill
each 'shellfish' cone with 2
tablespoons of prepared rice
mixture.

Plum Flower Egg

8 hard-cooked eggs, peeled
⅓ cup sugar
1½ teaspoons salt
red food coloring

*9½ inch square small bamboo
   mat (sudare) for rolling*

Makes about 16 'blossoms'.

Method
Separate egg whites and
yolks and work them sep-
arately through a sieve. Season yolks with 2 tablespoons
sugar and ¾ teaspoon salt.
Add remaining seasonings
to whites. To tint pink, blend
in a drop of red food coloring.

Cover the bamboo mat with
a clean cloth and spread it
evenly and firmly with the prepared egg whites, leaving a
border of about 1½ inches all
around. Work yolks into a roll
6 inches long and center on
the whites.

Using the cloth as a guide,
roll the egg white around the
yolk, enclosing it all in the
cloth. Secure by tying the
ends with string and roll this
firmly in the mat. Leave for
5–10 minutes, remove the
mat and set it aside.

Fit 5 chopsticks equi-
distantly around the cloth-
enclosed roll and secure
them with string, tied around
in several places.

Steam the roll for 15 minutes over boiling water on a
rack in a steamer or in a
colander placed over a saucepan. Cool the roll completely
and carefully remove the
chopsticks and cloth. Cut the
roll into slices about three-
eighths of an inch thick. The
slices, with their pink border
and yellow centers, resemble
plum flowers.

NEW YEAR

The New Year brings a feast
in boxes to the tables of
Japan. The foods are prepared
in advance and arranged
colorfully in nests of hand-
some lacquered containers
so that the housewife need
not cook for the duration of
the festival.

Each box is a repository for
a different kind of food. One
may contain sweets, another
broiled foods, and others
boiled preparations and vinegared mixtures of fish and
vegetables. The most famous
of the New Year prepara-
tions, however, cannot be
boxed.

Zoni
(Rice Cake Soup)

8 rice cakes, toasted
8 large shrimps, or 2 lobster
   tails (about ½ lb of either)
½ lb spinach leaves
2 taro or 1 medium sweet
   potato and 1 turnip, peeled
   and cut into ¼ inch thick
   slices
7 cups dashi (see page 49)
4 medium mushrooms
1 tablespoon Japanese soy
   sauce
⅛ teaspoon monosodium
   glutamate
lemon 'pine needles', cut from
   2 inch piece of thin lemon
   rind, ½ inch wide (see soup
garnishes, page 48)

Toasted rice cakes are obtain-
able in oriental stores.

Method
Peel the shrimps; if lobster
tails are used, leave them in
the shells.

Cook the shrimps in lightly

salted boiling water for 3
minutes; lobster tails require
a little longer cooking. Cut
lobster tails in half. Blanch the
spinach by pouring boiling
water over the leaves in a
saucepan. Drain and dry them
at once, and cut them into
slices 1 inch wide.

Simmer the taro (or sweet
potato and turnip) slices in
1 cup dashi for 10 minutes
or until tender. Drain and
reserve the liquid.

Trim off the mushroom
stems. In a saucepan heat ½
cup of the remaining dashi
and 1 teaspoon soy sauce
together and cook the mushroom caps in it for 5 minutes.
Drain and reserve the liquid.

In a saucepan combine the
reserved dashi used in cooking with the remaining 5½
cups of dashi and season the
broth with the remaining soy
sauce and monosodium
glutamate. Heat the broth
until steaming hot.

Arrange equal amounts of
the prepared vegetables and
shrimps or lobster tails in 4
individual bowls. Place 2 rice
cakes in each and fill the
bowls with the flavored hot
dashi. Float ¼ of the lemon
'pine needles' on the soup in
each bowl and serve at once.

OUTDOOR ENTERTAINING

Entertaining outdoors has its pleasures and pitfalls. The ambience comes ready-made with the setting of a pool, patio or barbecue, but the further the cook is from the kitchen, the more difficult it is to control the standard of the cooking. If you are planning an outdoor menu, don't be too ambitious — appetites are sharpened by fresh air and the simplest foods will be doubly welcome.

Choose simple, colorful dishes that will stand up well in the hot sun, and avoid aspics that will melt easily or delicate salads that can wilt. Select ingredients that are easy to carry; include, if you like, one or two cooked dishes that simply need reheating.

Set the table in as shady a spot as possible and be prepared with some kind of anchor for napkins and tablecloths that may blow in the wind. All dishes should be tightly covered until food is served. Provide a plentiful supply of ice for drinks.

The nearer you are to the kitchen, the more elaborate the menu can be, and chilled dishes are not only a refreshing contrast to the outdoor heat, but are also easy to prepare in advance.

The following three menus give suggestions for three outdoor parties — a barbecue, a buffet by the pool and an elegant patio dinner. Each menu serves 10 people.

An inviting barbecue includes juicy, char-broiled fillet steak, spiced spareribs, lamb chops filled with a mushroom stuffing and broiled onions. Savory side dishes of roasted ears of corn, garlic-stuffed tomatoes and potatoes à la Suisse complete the menu

MENU 1
Barbecue

Spiced Spareribs
Fillet Steak
Marchand de Vin
Lamb Chops with
Mushroom Stuffing
Broiled Onions
Roasted Corn in the Husk
Tomatoes Provençale
Potatoes à la Suisse
Pears in Red Currant Jelly
Watermelon Rafraîchis

TIMETABLE

Day before
Parboil spareribs, drain, cut in sections and store in refrigerator; make barbecue sauce. Make stuffing for lamb chops and keep tightly covered.

Morning
Pour marinade over steaks, cover and chill. Slice onions for broiling and cover tightly; prepare corn for roasting. Stuff tomatoes and arrange in dish ready for baking.
Scoop flesh from watermelon and chill melon basket. Macerate melon balls with remaining fruit in refrigerator. Prepare and poach pears in syrup, complete dish and chill.

Two or three hours before cooking
Stuff lamb chops and keep in refrigerator. Make and bake potatoes à la Suisse and cover with foil ready for reheating. Bake tomatoes and cover with foil ready for reheating.
Whip cream for pears and chill.
Arrange all food in dishes, ready for barbecuing and cover to carry to barbecue. Start cooking at 6:00 to serve barbecue at 7:30 p.m.

Order of Work
5–5:30
Light the barbecue.
Fill fruit into melon basket, cover, keep in refrigerator.
6:45
Lift fillet steaks from marinade and prepare sauce.
7:00
Set oven at moderate (350°F) and put in potatoes to reheat.
Roast corn on barbecue.
Broil onions and keep warm.
7:15
Put tomatoes in oven to reheat.
Barbecue lamb chops and spareribs.
7:20
Barbecue fillet steaks.
7:25
Transfer potatoes and tomatoes from oven to barbecue rack to keep hot.
7:30
Set pears and watermelon on a bed of ice on serving table.
7:30
Serve barbecue.

You will find that **cooking times** given in the individual recipes for these dishes have sometimes been adapted in the timetable to help you when cooking and serving this menu as a barbecue meal.

Spiced Spareribs

6 lb spareribs
1 onion, quartered
1 carrot quartered
1 stalk of celery, sliced
6 peppercorns
bouquet garni
salt

For barbecue sauce
$\frac{1}{4}$ cup soy sauce
$\frac{1}{2}$ cup dark brown sugar
$\frac{1}{4}$ cup sherry
$\frac{1}{2}$ teaspoon ground ginger
$\frac{1}{2}$ teaspoon ground allspice
$\frac{1}{4}$ teaspoon ground nutmeg

Method
Put the spareribs in a pan with the onion, carrot, celery, peppercorns, bouquet garni, a little salt and just enough water to cover. Add the lid, bring to a boil and simmer for 30 minutes or until almost tender. This preliminary cooking prevents the ribs from becoming dry during barbecuing. Cool the ribs, then drain them, and cut in 2–3 rib sections.

To make the sauce: combine the soy sauce, brown sugar, sherry and spices in a pan and heat gently, stirring, until the sugar dissolves; let cool.

To barbecue: brush the spareribs generously with sauce and cook 4–5 inches from glowing charcoal for 10–15 minutes or until they are crisp and browned. Turn them several times during cooking and brush often with sauce.

Fillet Steak Marchand de Vin

10 fillet steaks, cut 1 inch thick
oil or clarified butter
    (for brushing)

For sauce
2 cups red wine
6 shallots, finely chopped
1 clove of garlic, crushed
    (optional)
1 cup beef stock
bouquet garni
kneaded butter, made with
    2 tablespoons butter and
    1 tablespoon flour
1 tablespoon chopped parsley
salt and pepper

Method
Set the steaks in a shallow dish (not metal), pour over the wine, sprinkle with shallots, garlic, if used, and add bouquet garni. Cover and keep in the refrigerator for 3–6 hours, turning the steaks in the marinade from time to time. Remove the steaks and pat them dry.

To make the sauce: pour the marinade into a saucepan, add the stock and boil until reduced to about 2 cups; discard the bouquet garni. Add the kneaded butter to the sauce, a little at a time, and cook, stirring, until the sauce thickens – it should be the consistency of very thin cream. Taste for seasoning and keep warm. Add chopped parsley just before serving.

To broil the steaks: brush them with oil or melted clarified butter and cook 3–4 inches from glowing charcoal for 3–4 minutes on each side, turning the steaks once. Brush them often with oil or butter during cooking and sprinkle them with salt and pepper after turning. Serve the steaks with the sauce separately.

Lamb Chops with Mushroom Stuffing

10 thickly cut loin or rib lamb
   chops
oil or clarified butter
   (for brushing)

For stuffing
3 cups ($\frac{3}{4}$ lb) mushrooms,
   finely chopped
2 tablespoons butter
$\frac{1}{2}$ onion, finely chopped
1 clove of garlic, crushed
1 tablespoon chopped parsley
$\frac{1}{2}$ teaspoon thyme
salt and pepper

Trussing needle and string or
*   toothpicks*

Method
To make the stuffing: in a
skillet melt the butter, add the
onion and cook gently until
soft. Add the mushrooms and
cook, stirring, over high heat,
until all the moisture has
evaporated. Stir in the garlic,
cook 30 seconds longer, take
from the heat and add the
herbs with plenty of seasoning. Let cool.

With a small pointed knife,
cut as large a pocket as possible in each of the lamb
chops, fill them with the cool
stuffing and sew up with a
trussing needle and string or
fasten with toothpicks.
Watchpoint: do not stuff the
chops more than 2 hours
before cooking.

To broil: brush the chops
with oil or melted clarified
butter and cook 4–5 inches
from glowing charcoal for 7–
8 minutes on each side, turning the chops once. Brush the
chops often with oil or butter
during cooking and sprinkle
them with salt and pepper
after turning.

Broiled Onions

4–5 Bermuda or other large
   mild onions
oil or clarified butter
   (for brushing)
salt and pepper
2–3 teaspoons sugar

Method
Peel the onions and trim the
root neatly but do not remove
it. Cut the onions into thick
rounds through the root, so
the root holds the slices
together and they do not fall
apart.

Brush the slices with oil or
melted clarified butter, sprinkle
with salt, pepper and a little
sugar and set them, seasoned
side down, on a barbecue
rack. Broil until they are
browned and the sugar has
caramelized. Repeat the process on the other side.

Roasted Corn in the Husk

10–12 ears of corn
1 cup butter, softened
salt and pepper

Method
Strip back the husks from the
ears of corn and remove the
silk. Spread the kernels with
softened butter, sprinkle with
salt and pepper and pull up the
husks to cover the corn again,
tying the ends to keep them
in place. Soak the corn in
water for 10 minutes or until
the husks are saturated.

Roast the corn over char-
coal for 20–30 minutes or
until tender, turning from
time to time. Serve in the
husk.

Potatoes à la Suisse

4 lb potatoes
2 tablespoons butter
3 onions, thinly sliced
2 cups grated Gruyère cheese
salt
black pepper, freshly ground
4–5 cups stock

Method
Peel potatoes and cut them in
thin slices, about $\frac{1}{8}$ inch thick,
using a mandoline slicer, if
you like.

Spread one or two shallow
flameproof dishes with the
butter and arrange the potatoes in layers with the onions,
sprinkling each layer with
cheese and a little salt and
pepper and ending with a layer
of potatoes.

Sprinkle the top generously
with cheese and pour enough
stock down the sides of the
dish to come level with the
top layer of potatoes. Bake in
a moderately hot oven (375°F)
for 1 hour or until the potatoes
are tender and browned. Add
more stock during cooking if
the dish seems dry and cover
the potatoes if necessary to
prevent them from browning
too much.

Keep the potatoes hot in
the dish on the barbecue rack
until serving.

Tomatoes Provençale

6–8 vine-ripened tomatoes
6 tablespoons butter
1 onion, finely chopped
2 cloves of garlic, crushed
$\frac{1}{2}$ cup fresh white breadcrumbs
1 teaspoon thyme
salt and pepper

Method
Cut the tomatoes in half, crosswise, and squeeze out and
discard most of the seeds.

In a skillet melt the butter,
add the onion and cook until
soft. Stir in the garlic and
breadcrumbs and cook, stirring, until the breadcrumbs
are browned. Take from the
heat, add the thyme and
plenty of seasoning and spoon
the mixture into the tomatoes.

Set the tomatoes in a buttered shallow flameproof dish
and bake in a moderately hot
oven (375°F) for 12–15 minutes or until the tomatoes are
just tender. For serving keep
the tomatoes hot in the dish
on the barbecue rack.

To Clarify Butter
Cut regular butter into
medium-sized pieces and
melt in a thick saucepan
over low heat. Continue to
cook until the butter is
foaming well, pour into a
bowl and leave to settle.
Skim any foam from the
top and chill. The clarified
butter will form a solid
cake on top; discard liquid
beneath.

If not using at once,
melt it down, pour into a
covered container and
store in the refrigerator.

After roasting ears of corn in the husk, strip off the husks and serve corn with melted butter

Pears in red currant jelly are served with a bowl of whipped flavored cream separately

Pears in Red Currant Jelly

10–12 firm, ripe pears
3 cups red currant jelly
1½ cups sugar
3½ cups water
pared rind and juice of 3 lemons

For serving
1½ cups heavy cream, whipped until it holds a stiff shape
6 tablespoons brandy or 3 teaspoons vanilla
4 tablespoons sugar

This recipe was first given in Volume 7.

Method
To make the syrup: dissolve the sugar in the water, bring slowly to a boil, add the lemon juice and rind and simmer 5 minutes.

Keep the stems on the pears; pare them and remove the 'eye' from the bases. Place half the pears in prepared syrup, cover and poach them until tender. Even when the pears are ripe, this must take 20–30 minutes to prevent discoloration around the cores. Poach the remaining pears in the same way.

Drain the pears and arrange them in serving dishes. Boil the syrup until reduced to 1 cup. Add the red currant jelly, heat gently until dissolved and simmer the mixture until it is the consistency of maple syrup. Let cool to tepid, then spoon over the pears. Chill thoroughly.

Beat the brandy or vanilla and sugar into the whipped cream until the cream thickens again and serve separately.

Watermelon Rafraîchis

1 ripe watermelon
1 ripe honeydew or casaba melon
5 oranges
1 quart blackberries or black raspberries or 1 lb fresh Bing cherries, pitted – optional
⅓ cup sugar, or to taste
1 cup white wine
¼ cup Maraschino, Cointreau or Grand Marnier liqueur

Method
To make a watermelon basket for serving: cut 2 horizontal lengthwise slices almost to the center of the melon, then cut crosswise to meet them so 2 wedges of melon are removed, leaving a handle in the center. Scoop out the melon flesh with a ball cutter, discarding the seeds.

Halve the melon, discard the seeds and scoop out the flesh with a ball cutter. Cut the peel and pith from the oranges with a serrated-edge knife and section them (see box on page 44).

Add the oranges to the melon balls and blackberries, raspberries or cherries, if using. Sprinkle with sugar to taste, pour over the wine and liqueur, cover and chill at least 3 hours, stirring once or twice. Scrape any remaining flesh from the watermelon basket and chill the basket also.

Just before serving, pile the fruit in the melon basket, spoon over the juice and set the melon on a bed of crushed ice for serving.

Outdoor entertaining

*A basket carved from a watermelon is filled with a tempting array of chilled fruits —
melon balls, orange segments, fresh strawberries and cherries*

MENU 2
Poolside Buffet

Smoked Tongue Pâté
with Wholewheat Bread
Beef Roulade
Spinach and Bacon Salad
Eggplant Provençale
Fresh Peach Flan
Sangrià

TIMETABLE

Two or three days before
Make tongue pâté, seal and keep in refrigerator.

Day before
Make beef roulade, cool, strain sauce and keep meat and sauce in refrigerator. Make pastry dough for flans and keep in plastic bag in the refrigerator.

Morning
Wash spinach for salad and keep in plastic bag; fry and drain bacon; make dressing.
Make eggplant Provençale and chill. Line pastry dough into flan ring, bake blind and cool; soak macaroon crumbs.

An hour or two before serving
Take pâté from refrigerator, set crock or terrine on a board with wholewheat bread.
Slice beef roulade, arrange on platter, cover and keep in refrigerator. Pour sauce into a bowl for serving.
Complete peach flans.
Prepare and macerate fruits for sangrià; chill wine and soda.

Just before serving
Toss spinach and bacon with dressing. Complete the sangrià. Carry dishes to buffet table.

You will find that **cooking times** given in the individual recipes for these dishes have sometimes been adapted in the timetable to help you when cooking and serving this menu as a buffet.

Smoked Tongue Pâté

1 lb cooked, pickled or smoked beef tongue
$1\frac{1}{2}$ cups clarified butter (see page 62)
$\frac{1}{2}$ teaspoon ground mace
black pepper, freshly ground (to taste)

Crock or terrine mold (1 quart capacity)

Method
Work the tongue through the fine blade of a grinder and beat in 1 cup of clarified butter. Alternatively, purée the tongue with the butter in a blender, working half the mixture at a time. Beat the mace and plenty of pepper into the tongue mixture and pack it into the crock or terrine, making sure all air is excluded.

Melt the remaining clarified butter, pour it over the tongue and keep in the refrigerator at least 3 days so the flavor mellows before using. The pâté can be kept up to 1 month in the refrigerator if the butter seal is unbroken. Serve at room temperature with wholewheat bread.

Beef Roulade

2 round steaks (about 2 lb each)
2 tablespoons oil
2 carrots, diced
2 onions, diced
2 stalks of celery, diced
1 cup red wine
1 cup stock
bouquet garni
1 teaspoon tomato paste
bunch of watercress (for garnish)

For filling
2 lb ground beef
2 tablespoons butter
2 onions, finely chopped
1 cup fresh white breadcrumbs
3 cloves of garlic, crushed
grated rind of 2 lemons
3 tablespoons chopped parsley
salt and pepper
2 eggs, beaten to mix
8 hard-cooked eggs
$\frac{1}{2}$ lb cooked tongue, cut in strips
$\frac{1}{2}$ lb cooked ham, cut in strips

Trussing needle and string

Method
Discard any bone and cut the fat and skin from the edge of the steaks. Place them between 2 sheets of wax paper and pound them with a mallet or rolling pin to about $\frac{3}{8}$ inch thickness.

To make the filling: melt the butter and fry the chopped onion until soft but not browned. In a bowl mix the onion with the ground beef, breadcrumbs, garlic, lemon rind, parsley and plenty of seasoning. Stir in the 2 beaten eggs to bind the mixture.

Slice the hard-cooked eggs. Spread the beef mixture on the round steak and scatter the strips of ham and tongue over it. Lay the slices of egg on top, sprinkle with seasoning and roll up each piece of steak to enclose the filling; sew with a trussing needle and string.

Refreshing as the pool itself, a feast of stuffed beef roulades, smoked tongue pâté and a casserole of eggplant Provençale is accompanied by a loaf of homemade wholewheat bread and a thirst-quenching pitcher of sangrià

In a flameproof casserole heat the oil and brown the beef rolls on all sides over medium heat. Take out, add the carrots, onions and celery, cover the pan, lower the heat and cook 5–7 minutes or until the vegetables are soft. Replace the meat, pour in the wine and stock, add the bouquet garni, tomato paste and seasoning and cover the pan.

Braise the beef rolls in a moderate oven (350°F) for $1\frac{1}{2}$–$1\frac{3}{4}$ hours or until a skewer inserted in the center of a roll for 1 minute is hot to the touch when withdrawn. Let the rolls cool in the pan until tepid, then take out and chill.

To serve: discard the strings from the rolls, cut them in $\frac{1}{2}$ inch slices and arrange, overlapping, on a platter. Garnish the dish with watercress.

Spinach and Bacon Salad

2–2½ lb fresh spinach
½ lb bacon, diced

For dressing
½ cup olive oil
2 tablespoons lemon juice
black pepper, freshly ground
salt (optional)

Method

Wash the spinach thoroughly, discarding the stems, and drain. Fry the bacon until crisp and drain on paper towels.

To make the dressing: whisk the oil and lemon juice together with plenty of pepper.

A short time before serving, toss the salad with the dressing, scatter over the bacon and taste the salad for seasoning – salt may or may not be needed, depending on the saltiness of the bacon.

Eggplant Provençale

4 medium eggplants, sliced
½ cup olive oil
6 tomatoes, peeled, seeded and cut in strips
2 cloves of garlic, crushed
1 tablespoon chopped parsley
1 teaspoon thyme
½ teaspoon basil
salt and pepper
¼ cup browned breadcrumbs

Method

Sprinkle the eggplant slices with salt, cover and let stand 30 minutes to draw out the bitter juices (dégorger). Rinse the slices with cold water and pat dry with paper towels.

In a skillet heat ⅓ cup of the oil and fry the eggplant slices a few at a time to brown them on both sides; take out and reserve.

Add another tablespoon of oil to the pan, put in the tomatoes and garlic and cook 2–3 minutes; take from the heat and stir in the herbs and salt and pepper to taste.

Arrange the eggplant slices, overlapping, in an oiled baking dish and spread the tomato mixture on top. Sprinkle with breadcrumbs and the remaining oil and bake in a moderate oven (350°F) for 30 minutes or until the eggplant is very tender. Let cool and serve in the baking dish.

Fresh Peach Flan

French flan pastry, made with 3¾ cups flour, 1 cup butter, 1 cup sugar, 8 egg yolks and 2 teaspoons vanilla (see Volume 3)
10–12 large macaroons, crushed
4–6 tablespoons kirsch or Maraschino liqueur
8–9 fresh peaches or 2 cans (16 oz each) peach halves
¼ cup orange juice or juice from canned peaches
1½ cups apricot jam glaze

Two 9 inch flan rings

Method

Make the French flan pastry dough and chill 30 minutes. Roll it out, line the flan rings and bake blind in a moderately hot oven (375°F) for 15–20 minutes or until the pastry is lightly browned.

Spoon the kirsch or Maraschino liqueur and orange or peach juice over the macaroons and let soak.

If using fresh peaches, scald, peel and halve them, discarding the pits; drain canned peaches. Spread the soaked macaroon crumbs in the cool flan shells and arrange the halves on top. Brush the peaches and pastry generously with hot apricot jam glaze and transfer the flans to platters to serve.

Sangrià

3 bottles full-bodied red wine
½ cup brandy
juice of 2 lemons
1 lemon, sliced
¼ cup sugar (or to taste)
1–2 quarts club soda, chilled
fruits for garnish – hulled strawberries, pitted cherries, sliced pineapple, sliced orange (optional)

Method

Put the fruits for garnish, if using, in a large pitcher or punch bowl, pour over the brandy, cover and let macerate 1–2 hours.

A short time before serving, pour in the wine and lemon juice, add the lemon slices and sugar to taste; chill.

Just before serving, add chilled club soda and ice cubes to dilute the sangrià to taste.

Sangrià, filled with fresh fruits, is an ideal drink for outdoor entertaining

MENU 3
Candlelight Dinner

Chilled Watercress Soup
Cheese Straws
Stuffed Squabs en Cocotte with Olives
Tomato and Artichoke Heart Salad
Iced Caramel Pecan Mousse

TIMETABLE

Day before
Make and bake cheese straws and keep in an airtight container.
Make stuffing for squabs and keep in refrigerator.
If using fresh artichoke hearts, cook them; make dressing.
Make iced caramel pecan mousses and keep in freezer.

Morning
Make the watercress soup and chill.
Stuff and truss squabs.
Peel tomatoes for salad and keep covered.

Assemble ingredients for final cooking from 7:00 for dinner around 8 p.m.

You will find that **cooking times** given in the individual recipes for these dishes have sometimes been adapted in the timetable to help you when cooking and serving this menu as a party meal.

Order of Work
7:00
If using oven, set at moderate (350°F).
Brown squabs and cook on top of stove or in heated oven.
Decorate mousses and replace in freezer.
7:30
Put extra stuffing in oven to reheat with squabs.
Mix salad dressing and keep covered in refrigerator.
Pour soup into bowls and keep in refrigerator; arrange cheese straws on a platter.
7:45
Reheat stuffing over low heat on top of stove if not using oven.
Transfer squabs to platter and keep warm.
Make sauce, spoon over squabs, pile extra stuffing on dish and keep warm.
8:00
Serve soup.
Top mousses with strawberries just before serving.

Chilled Watercress Soup

3 bunches of watercress
2 tablespoons butter
3 medium potatoes, thinly sliced
6 cups chicken stock
3 cups heavy cream
salt and pepper

Method
Chop the watercress leaves and stems, reserving a few leaves for garnish.

In a kettle melt the butter, add the watercress and potatoes, cover the pan and cook gently for 12—15 minutes or until the vegetables are very soft. Pour in the stock, bring to a boil, season and simmer 10—15 minutes, stirring occasionally.

Cool the soup slightly, then work it through a sieve or food mill or purée it in a blender. Return it to the pan with the cream, bring just to a boil and taste for seasoning. The soup should be the consistency of very thin cream because it will thicken on cooling; if necessary, add a little more stock. Cover the soup tightly, let cool, then chill it.

For serving, top each bowl with a few leaves of watercress and serve cheese straws separately.

Cheese Straws

Set the oven at moderately hot (375°F).

With the fingertips rub 6 tablespoons butter into 1 cup flour until the mixture crumbs. Stir in $\frac{1}{2}$ cup grated Parmesan or dry Cheddar cheese.

Mix 1 egg yolk with 1 tablespoon water and stir into the cheese mixture to form a dough, adding $\frac{1}{2}$—1 tablespoon more water if neces-

sary. Knead lightly until dough is smooth, wrap tightly and chill at least 1 hour.

Roll out the dough to about $\frac{1}{4}$ inch thickness, brush with glaze made of 1 egg, beaten to mix with $\frac{1}{2}$ teaspoon salt, and cut into even strips $\frac{1}{4}$ inch wide and 4 inches long.

Lay the dough strips on a baking sheet, twist them, pressing down the ends firmly, and sprinkle with poppyseeds. Bake in the heated oven for 12—15 minutes or until the straws are golden brown. Cool on the baking sheet.

Stuffed Squabs en Cocotte with Olives

10 squabs
2 cups pitted green olives
2 tablespoons oil
2 tablespoons butter
2 cups white wine
2 cups chicken stock
salt and pepper
2 tablespoons arrowroot, mixed to a paste with 2 tablespoons water
2 tablespoons chopped parsley

For stuffing
$2\frac{1}{2}$ cups cracked wheat (bulgur)
2 eggs, beaten to mix
5 cups chicken stock or water
1 cup pine nuts
1 cup ($\frac{1}{3}$ lb) dried apricots

Trussing needle and string

Method
Pour boiling water to cover over the dried apricots, let stand 15 minutes, drain and chop them coarsely.

To make the stuffing: put the cracked wheat in a heavy flameproof casserole with the eggs and cook over medium heat for 8—12 minutes, stirring constantly, until all the egg is absorbed and the wheat is dry and granular. Pour in the chicken stock or water, stir in the chopped apricots, pine nuts and seasoning and bring to a boil.

Cover the pot and simmer on top of the stove or bake in a moderate oven (350°F) for 20–25 minutes or until all the liquid is absorbed and the cracked wheat is tender. Let cool with the lid on.

Spoon the stuffing into the squabs and truss them. Pile any remaining stuffing into a buttered baking dish, cover and reheat to serve with the squabs.

In a large shallow flame-proof casserole or roasting pan heat the oil and butter and brown the squabs on all sides. Pour in 1 cup wine and 1 cup stock, season, add the casserole lid or cover the roasting pan tightly with foil and bake in a moderately hot oven (375°F) for 30 minutes or until the squabs are tender when pierced with a skewer.

Take out the squabs, remove the trussing strings, arrange the birds on a platter and keep warm.

Discard the fat from the casserole or pan, leaving the pan juices, and add the remaining wine and stock with the olives. Boil until it is reduced to about 3 cups, then add the arrowroot paste and stir just until the sauce thickens.

Take from the heat, taste for seasoning and spoon a little of the sauce over the squabs. Pile any remaining stuffing down one side of the dish, sprinkle the squabs with pars-ley and serve the remaining sauce separately.

Cheese straws are delicious accompaniments to soups

Tomato and Artichoke Salad

2 boxes cherry tomatoes,
  peeled
10–12 fresh baby globe
  artichokes, cooked (see
  right) or 2 packages frozen
  globe artichokes, cooked
  according to package
  directions and drained
4 shallots, finely chopped
2 tablespoons chopped
  parsley
2 teaspoons chopped fresh
  tarragon, basil or chives
½ cup oil
2 tablespoons lemon juice
salt and pepper

If fresh herbs are not available,
omit them from the recipe.

Method
Whisk the oil and lemon juice
until slightly thickened and
stir in the shallots with herbs
and seasoning to taste.

Put the artichokes and
tomatoes in a shallow salad
bowl or serving dish, spoon
over the dressing, cover and
chill thoroughly before serving.

*To test if the artichoke is
cooked, pull off a leaf; if it
comes away easily, it is ready*

To Prepare
Fresh
Artichoke Hearts

Cut the stems from baby
artichokes and trim the tops
of the leaves, leaving about
1 inch. Cook the artichokes in
boiling salted water for 15–20
minutes or until tender. If a
leaf pulls away easily, the artichoke is cooked. Drain and
refresh them.

Cut the artichokes in half or
quarters or leave them whole,
according to size. If the artichokes are very small, they
are completely edible, but a
little of the hairy choke of
larger ones may need to be
discarded.

Iced Caramel
Pecan Mousse

2 cups coarsely chopped
  pecans
2 cups sugar
2 cups heavy cream, whipped
  until it holds a soft shape
2 envelopes of gelatin, soaked
  in ½ cup water

For meringue Italienne
5 egg whites
1 cup sugar
½ cup water

For decoration
½ cup heavy cream, stiffly
  whipped
10 fresh strawberries

*10 ramekins or individual
  soufflé dishes; pastry bag
  and medium star tube*

Method
Prepare the dishes with a
collar of wax paper or foil to
extend 1½–2 inches above the
edge of the dish and tie them
with string. Oil a baking sheet.

In a heavy skillet put the 2
cups sugar and heat gently,
stirring occasionally, until
melted and the sugar has
started to caramelize. Stir in
the pecans and cook the mixture, stirring, to a rich golden
brown. At once pour onto the
baking sheet and leave until
cold and hard. Crush the mixture in a mortar and pestle or
with a rolling pin in a bowl so
it remains fairly coarse.

To make the meringue
Italienne: heat sugar with the
water until dissolved, bring to
a boil and boil until the syrup
forms a firm, pliable ball when
dropped in cold water (250°F
on a sugar thermometer).
Meanwhile, beat the egg
whites until they hold a stiff
peak and, when the syrup is
ready, pour it gradually onto
the egg whites, beating constantly. Continue beating until

the meringue is cool and very
stiff. Dissolve the gelatin in
the water over gentle heat,
cool and add to the meringue.
Fold in two-thirds of the
crushed caramel mixture, followed by the lightly whipped
cream.

Watchpoint: the meringue
mixture must be cool before
the cream is added, otherwise
the cream will melt.

Spoon the mixture into the
prepared dishes to come at
least 1 inch above the rim of
the dishes; freeze for 5 hours
or until very firm. Keep the
remaining caramel mixture in
an airtight container for
decoration.

To finish the mousses: peel
off the paper collars and press
the reserved crushed caramel
around the edge. Using a
pastry bag fitted with a
medium star tube, pipe a
rosette of stiffly whipped
cream in the center of each
mousse. Keep the mousses in
the freezer until serving, then
top each rosette with a fresh
strawberry.

Outdoor entertaining

Iced caramel pecan mousse is an impressive finale to a candle-light patio dinner

Mushrooms in white wine are served with fingers of toast spread with anchovy butter (recipe is on page 76)

Mushrooms in white wine begin a cold menu that is easy to make in advance. Or, if you prefer, serve the mushrooms as a salad with the entrée of chicken coated with tuna sauce. If you'd like a hot appetizer, there's an unusual green soup flavored with watercress, spinach and herbs. Dessert is a delicious galette Normande of crisp pastry layered with apples.

Both the appetizer and the entrée will be enhanced by the company of a good wine. But something out of the ordinary is called for by the salty tang of the anchovy butter with the mushrooms and the tuna sauce on the chicken. A happy solution might be a dry yet aromatic white in the Eastern European tradition, like Sipon from Mariber in Yugoslavia. Alternatively you could try that unique variety called Green Hungarian, now available from the better California vintners.

PREPARE AHEAD FOR A PARTY

Mushrooms in White Wine
or
Potage Vert (Green Soup)

Chicken with Tuna

Galette Normande

White wine – Sipon (Yugoslavia)
or Green Hungarian (California)

TIMETABLE

Day before
Cook chicken with vegetables, wine and bouquet garni. Let cool in the liquid, then drain and keep tightly covered in refrigerator. Discard bouquet garni and keep tuna in liquid in refrigerator. Make vinaigrette dressing for chicken accompaniments.
Prepare pastry dough for galette Normande, wrap in plastic bag and chill. Make filling for galette and store in refrigerator in covered container.

Morning
Cook mushrooms in wine and store covered, in refrigerator in a serving dish. *Make soup but do not add lemon juice or liaison.*
Cut up chicken, discarding skin, and keep covered in refrigerator; make tuna sauce and keep covered.
Cook rice, drain, dry and keep covered; cook beans, drain and cool; slice tomatoes and keep covered.
Chop mint for chicken and parsley for mushrooms and slice onions.
Roll out pastry dough for galette and bake. Cool rounds, then ice one round and keep remainder in airtight container.

Assemble ingredients for final cooking from 7:20 for dinner around 8 p.m.

Order of Work
7:20
Assemble layers of galette with apple filling; set on a platter.
7:30
Mix rice for chicken with vinaigrette dressing, arrange on a platter, coat chicken with sauce and keep in refrigerator.
Mix vegetables with dressing and keep separately.
Make toast, cut in fingers, spread with anchovy butter and keep warm or heat rolls.
7:50
If serving mushrooms hot, reheat in a saucepan over moderate heat, transfer to a hot dish and serve, or sprinkle cold mushrooms with parsley and serve.
Reheat soup, add liaison and lemon juice, taste for seasoning and serve at once.
8:00
Serve appetizer.

You will find that **cooking times** given in the individual recipes for these dishes have sometimes been adapted in the timetable to help you when cooking and serving this menu as a party meal.

Appetizer

Mushrooms in White Wine

4 cups (1 lb) mushrooms
3 tablespoons butter or olive oil
2 large onions, thinly sliced
1 cup white wine
bouquet garni
salt
black pepper, freshly ground
1 tablespoon chopped parsley

To serve
fingers of toast spread with anchovy or crisp rolls and unsalted butter

If you prefer the mushrooms in white wine cold, serve them as an accompaniment to the chicken instead of a separate appetizer.

Method
Trim the mushrooms and wipe them with a damp cloth. Cut them in thick slices and sauté in the butter or olive oil for 1–2 minutes, stirring. Remove from the pan, reduce the heat, add the onions and cook slowly until they are soft but not brown. Pour on the white wine, add bouquet garni and simmer until wine is reduced by half.

Return mushrooms to the pan, season and simmer 5 minutes. Discard the bouquet garni and pour the mushroom mixture into a gratin or serving dish. Sprinkle with parsley and serve hot or chilled.

Serve with fingers of hot toast spread with anchovy butter or hot crisp rolls and unsalted butter.

Slice the onions thinly and mushrooms thickly for mushrooms in white wine

Add the sautéed mushrooms to the onions and wine

Anchovy Butter

Cream 2 tablespoons unsalted butter on a plate with a metal spatula. In a mortar and pestle crush or pound 2–3 anchovy fillets, soaked in milk to remove excess salt. Work anchovy with the butter and freshly ground black pepper. Blend in 1 teaspoon anchovy paste to accent the flavor and give the butter a delicate pink color.

Potage vert (green soup) is garnished with a spoonful of cream stirred in before serving

Alternative appetizer

Potage Vert
(Green Soup)

bunch of scallions, trimmed
  and finely chopped
bunch of watercress, washed
  and chopped
$\frac{1}{2}$ lb fresh spinach, thoroughly
  washed, stems removed and
  leaves chopped
$\frac{1}{4}$ cup chopped parsley
2 cups chicken stock
2 cups stock (made with a ham
  bone) or 2 cups additional
  chicken stock
pepper
salt (optional)
3 egg yolks
$\frac{3}{4}$ cup heavy cream
squeeze of lemon juice

Method
Combine the chicken and ham
stock (if using), bring to a boil
and add the chopped vege-
tables and parsley. Season
with pepper and salt, if not
using ham stock, and simmer
gently for 15–20 minutes.
Work the mixture through a
sieve or purée in a blender,
return soup to pan and reheat.

Mix egg yolks with $\frac{1}{2}$ cup
cream, stir in a little of the hot
soup and add this liaison to
remaining soup. Heat gently,
stirring, until soup thickens
slightly but do not boil. Serve
at once; add a spoonful of
cream to each bowl as garnish.

To Heat Small Rolls
The best way to heat small
rolls so they become crisp
on the outside but not
hard is to put them in a
paper bag and heat them
in a hot oven (400°F) for
4–5 minutes.

For chicken with tuna, chicken pieces are arranged on a bed of rice, coated with sauce and surrounded by the colorful tomato, green bean and herb garnish

Entrée

Chicken
with Tuna

$3\frac{1}{2}$–4 lb roasting chicken
1 can ($6\frac{1}{2}$ oz) tuna in oil,
    drained and flaked
1 onion, stuck with a clove
1 carrot
$\frac{1}{2}$ cup white wine
1 cup water
bouquet garni
1 stalk of celery
salt and pepper
$\frac{3}{4}$ cup mayonnaise
squeeze of lemon juice
$\frac{1}{2}$ cup heavy cream, whipped
    until it holds a soft shape

To serve
1 cup rice
$\frac{3}{4}$ lb green beans, trimmed and
    cut in half
about $\frac{1}{2}$ cup vinaigrette
    dressing
1 teaspoon paprika
3 ripe tomatoes, peeled and
    thinly sliced
1 teaspoon chopped mint
1 tablespoon chopped parsley
pinch of oregano

Method
Put the chicken, onion, carrot, wine, water, bouquet garni and celery together in a large pan. Season and add the tuna. Cover pan and simmer for about 1 hour, turning chicken occasionally while it cooks, until the chicken is tender and no pink juice runs out when the thigh is pierced with a fork. Let the chicken cool in the liquid.

Cook the rice in plenty of boiling salted water for 12 minutes or until tender. Drain well, rinse with hot water, drain again and spread out in a warm place to dry. Cook the beans in boiling salted water for 15 minutes or until tender;

drain, refresh and drain again.

Remove chicken from the pan and cut it in 5 pieces, discarding the skin.

Discard bouquet garni and vegetables from the pan; strain tuna from liquid and reserve both tuna and liquid.

To make the sauce: pound the tuna in a mortar and pestle and beat the tuna purée into the mayonnaise with the lemon juice. Alternatively, purée the tuna with the mayonnaise and lemon juice in a blender. Fold in the lightly whipped cream. If necessary, thin the sauce to a coating consistency with a little of the reserved cooking liquid.

Stir the paprika into about two-thirds of the vinaigrette dressing and mix with the cooked rice. Spoon rice down center of a serving dish, arrange the chicken pieces on top and spoon over just enough tuna sauce to coat the pieces. Pour remaining sauce into a sauce boat.

Carefully mix beans and tomatoes with remaining vinaigrette dressing, add mint, parsley and oregano, arrange on either side of chicken, and serve the dish chilled.

Beat the pounded tuna into the mayonnaise with the lemon juice for chicken with tuna

Gently mix the sliced tomatoes and green bean garnish with vinaigrette dressing

Dessert

Galette Normande

For Danish shortcake pastry
2 cups flour
¾ cup butter
¾ cup confectioners' sugar
2 egg yolks
1 teaspoon vanilla

For apple filling
6–7 medium-sized tart apples
1 tablespoon butter
grated rind of ½ lemon
about ½ cup sugar

For icing
6 tablespoons confectioners'
  sugar
about 2 tablespoons water or
  sugar syrup (made with
  2 tablespoons sugar and
  2 tablespoons water)
½ teaspoon vanilla
2 tablespoons red currant jelly

Paper decorating cone

Method
Set oven at moderately hot
(375°F).
  To make Danish shortcake
pastry: sift flour onto a board
or marble slab and make a
large well in the center. Add
butter, confectioners' sugar,
egg yolks and vanilla and work
together with the fingertips
until smooth. Gradually draw
in flour, working with the
whole hand to form a smooth
dough. Chill 1 hour.
  To prepare the apple filling:
wipe skins of apples with a
damp cloth, cut in quarters
and remove the cores. Butter
a large pan and slice the
apples into it. Cover with a
sheet of buttered foil and a
lid and cook gently until
apples are pulpy.
  Work apples through a fine
sieve or food mill and return

purée to pan with lemon rind
and sugar. Boil rapidly until
mixture is very thick, stirring
constantly to prevent sticking,
but be careful as mixture is
likely to splash. Alternatively,
cook mixture, uncovered, in a
casserole in a moderately hot
oven (375°F) until thick. Then
spread out on a plate to cool.
  Divide pastry dough into
thirds; roll each piece into an
8 inch circle and transfer the
rounds to baking sheets. Prick
dough with a fork and bake in
heated oven 10–12 minutes
or until the pastry is delicately
browned. Trim rounds to neat
circles with a knife while still
warm, then cool them. Sandwich cooled rounds with apple
filling.
  Beat red currant jelly until
smooth and soft. Put into a
paper decorating cone and
cut a little piece from the tip
so jelly pipes in a thin line.
  To make the icing: mix the
confectioners' sugar with the
vanilla and enough sugar
syrup or water to make a
paste. Heat this gently to
tepid over a pan of hot water –
it should just coat the back of
the spoon – then spread
quickly over pastry round.
  Decorate the galette at
once with red currant jelly
piped into neat parallel lines,
then draw a skewer or the
point of a paring knife across
the jelly lines in alternate
directions to make a zig-zag
pattern.

Sandwich the three shortcake pastry rounds with apple filling for the galette

After piping red currant jelly on icing, mark surface with point of a knife to give zig-zag effect

Galette Normande is sandwiched with apple filling and coated with icing.
To decorate, red currant jelly lines are piped on top and marked in a zig-zag pattern

Individual fish molds are served with a white sauce (recipe is on page 85)

HOT SAVORY MOLDS

Delicious savory molds can be made from all kinds of ingredients like eggplant, cauliflower, raw veal or haddock fillet. These light, creamy mixtures are poured into one large or several smaller individual molds and steamed or cooked in a water bath.

Fish, chicken and meat are used raw, except for ham, which would be too salty if it were not previously cooked. A panada (used to bind the mixture together) is always added and this may be a thick white sauce, soaked breadcrumbs or unbeaten egg whites.

If working by hand, to achieve the right smooth, soft consistency, fish and meat must be pounded thoroughly in a mortar and pestle, before mixing with the panada, or you can improvise with the end of a rolling pin and a sturdy bowl. Vegetables must be cooked first, then made into a purée.

To save time, many fish, meat and chicken mixtures can be worked in a blender with the panada, instead of pounding them first in a mortar and pestle. Cream and butter are often added to enrich the mixture, which should be well seasoned. Some fish or meat molds may be filled with a salpicon (a shredded mixture bound with a sauce) for extra flavor.

Savory molds rise very little during cooking, so the mold or pan should be filled to within $\frac{1}{4}$ inch of the top. When the mixture is cooked, it shrinks from the sides of the mold and is firm to the touch. Most savory molds are coated with béchamel sauce or a sauce of contrasting flavor before serving.

83

To Steam a Mold

The easiest way is to use a special steamer, or a covered metal colander over a pan of hot water. The mold is placed in the top part of the steamer so that steam rising from hot water in the bottom cooks the mold by moist heat. You can also steam by placing the mold on a wire rack above a shallow layer of water in a covered kettle.

To Cook in a Water Bath

Set mold or pan in a roasting pan of hot water, deep enough to come at least halfway up sides of mold or pan. Place roasting pan with mold or pan in a moderate oven (350°F) to cook for time stated in recipe.

To Turn out a Savory Mold

A hot savory mold should slip easily out of its mold or pan. To turn out: place a dish over the top of the mold or pan, invert it and the mold will slide out onto the dish.

Where recipes use **tomato paste**, you may substitute **tomato purée** by increasing the quantity proportionately.

As a guide, 1 tablespoon tomato purée equals 1 teaspoon tomato paste with 2 teaspoons water.

Cauliflower Mold

1 large or 2 small cauliflowers
1 bay leaf
1 tablespoon butter

For panada
thick béchamel sauce, made with 3 tablespoons butter, 3 tablespoons flour, 1 cup milk (infused with slice of onion, 6 peppercorns, blade of mace and bay leaf)
salt and pepper
pinch of ground mace
2 eggs, one separated
1 tablespoon heavy cream
4–6 large spinach leaves
2 cups duxelles sauce (see right) or simple tomato sauce (see page 87)

6–7 inch springform pan

Method
Break the cauliflower into flowerets, including a few of the leaves and all of the stalk. Cook these with bay leaf in boiling salted water for 8–10 minutes or until tender. Drain cauliflower well, discard bay leaf and work through a food mill or sieve or purée in a blender.

Return cauliflower to the pan with the butter and dry over low heat, stirring until the purée is firm. Reserve.

Butter the springform pan. Dip spinach leaves in boiling water for a few seconds to make them pliable and cut away the stalks. Drain them well and line pan with them, shiny side of leaves down.

Stir cauliflower purée into béchamel sauce, season well and add the mace. Beat in the whole egg and egg yolk with cream. Beat egg white until it holds a stiff peak and fold into mixture.

Transfer mixture at once to the prepared pan to within $\frac{1}{4}$ inch of the top, cover with foil and steam on top of the stove or cook in a water bath in a moderate oven (350°F) for 35–40 minutes or until firm to the touch.

Let mold stand 1–2 minutes in a warm place, then turn out onto a hot serving platter. Spoon around a little of the duxelles or tomato sauce; serve the rest separately.

Duxelles Sauce

2 shallots or small onions, finely chopped
$\frac{1}{4}$ cup butter
1 cup ($\frac{1}{4}$ lb) mushrooms, finely chopped
3 tablespoons flour
2 cups veal or chicken stock
2 teaspoons chopped parsley
1 teaspoon mixed herbs (chives, tarragon, thyme)
salt and pepper

Makes 2 cups.

Method
Melt 2 tablespoons butter in a pan, add onion or shallot and cook until soft. Add remaining butter with mushrooms and cook over medium heat, stirring occasionally, for 3–4 minutes or until all moisture has evaporated.

Take from heat, stir in the flour, pour in the stock, bring to a boil, stirring, add herbs and season well. Simmer 1–2 minutes and serve.

Eggplant Mold

2 large eggplants ($\frac{3}{4}$–1 lb each), peeled and diced
1 cup ($\frac{1}{2}$ lb) chopped ham (half fat, half lean)
1 tablespoon chopped parsley
4 eggs, separated
thick béchamel sauce, made with 3 tablespoons butter, $2\frac{1}{2}$ tablespoons flour, 1 cup milk (infused with slice of onion, 6 peppercorns, blade of mace, bay leaf)
$\frac{1}{2}$ cup grated Gruyère cheese
salt and pepper
2 cups simple tomato sauce (for serving – see page 87)

6 inch charlotte mold or soufflé dish (1$\frac{1}{2}$ quart capacity)

Method
Cook eggplant in boiling salted water for 4–5 minutes or until barely tender. Drain thoroughly, mash and drain again, if necessary; eggplant must be quite dry. Add the chopped ham and parsley.

Set oven at hot (400°F) and butter the mold or dish.

Stir egg yolks into béchamel sauce and add to eggplant mixture with cheese and plenty of seasoning. Beat egg whites until they hold a stiff peak and fold into eggplant mixture.

Transfer to prepared mold or dish to within $\frac{1}{4}$ inch of the top and bake in heated oven for 25–30 minutes or until well browned. Serve from mold or dish in which it was cooked or turn out onto a hot platter and pour around a little of the tomato sauce, serving the rest separately.

Zucchini Mold

Trim $1\frac{1}{2}$ lb small zucchini, slice them thinly, then follow the same recipe as for eggplant mold.

Individual Fish Molds

1 lb haddock fillet
béchamel sauce, made with
   3 tablespoons butter,
   3 tablespoons flour, $1\frac{1}{4}$ cups
   milk (infused with slice of
   onion, 6 peppercorns, blade
   of mace and bay leaf)
2 eggs
$\frac{1}{4}$ lb cooked, peeled baby
   shrimps or chopped medium
   shrimps
3 tablespoons heavy cream
salt and pepper
7–8 small mushrooms
squeeze of lemon juice
1 tablespoon butter

For white sauce
$\frac{1}{4}$ cup butter
3 tablespoons flour
$1\frac{1}{2}$ cups milk

7–8 individual dariole molds
or custard cups

Method
Remove any skin and bones from the fish and pass it twice through the fine blade of a grinder.

Pound the fish in a mortar and pestle. Add cooled béchamel sauce gradually, beating well. Or, instead of pounding, the ground fish and sauce can be worked in a blender for a few seconds only until just smooth. Beat in the eggs, add shrimps and cream and season well.

Trim mushroom stalks level with the caps and cook with lemon juice and butter and 1 tablespoon water until

For individual fish molds, add béchamel sauce to uncooked, pounded haddock and beat together; beat in the eggs and cooked chopped shrimps

Put the fish mixture into the buttered molds, each with a mushroom on the bottom, and poach them

tender. Drain and reserve.

Butter molds or cups, place a mushroom in the bottom of each and fill to within $\frac{1}{4}$ inch of the tops with fish mixture. Cover each mold or cup with a piece of foil and steam on top of the stove or cook in a water bath in a moderate oven (350°F) for 20–25 minutes or until quite firm to the touch.

Meanwhile make the white sauce and season well.

Let molds stand 1–2 minutes in a warm place, then turn out onto a hot platter. Spoon around a little of the white sauce and serve the rest separately.

Salmon Mold

$1\frac{1}{2}$ lb fresh salmon fillets or
   salmon steaks
2 eggs, beaten to mix
6 tablespoons heavy cream

For panada
$\frac{1}{4}$ cup butter
1 cup milk
6 tablespoons flour
salt and pepper

For white wine sauce
1 cup white wine
1 shallot, finely chopped
2 tablespoons butter
2 tablespoons flour
1 cup fish stock or $\frac{1}{2}$ cup
   clam juice and $\frac{1}{2}$ cup water
   (mixed)
1 egg yolk
6 tablespoons heavy cream

To garnish
2 cucumbers
1 tablespoon butter
1 tablespoon chopped fresh
   dill (optional)

7 inch springform pan,
kugelhopf or ring mold
($1\frac{1}{2}$ quart capacity)

Method
Remove any skin and bones from salmon and chop flesh.

Butter the pan or mold.

To make the panada: melt the butter in the milk and bring just to a boil; take pan from heat, add flour all at once and beat until mixture is smooth and pulls away from the sides of the pan. Season and cool. Pound fish in a mortar and pestle until

smooth, then work in panada a little at a time. Or, instead of pounding, work chopped fish and panada for a few seconds in a blender until just smooth. Beat in the eggs and cream and adjust seasoning.

Spoon the mixture into the prepared mold or pan to within $\frac{1}{4}$ inch of the top, cover with foil and steam on top of the stove or cook in a water bath in a moderate oven (350°F) for 40 minutes or until mixture is firm to the touch.

To prepare the white wine sauce: put wine and shallot in a small pan and boil until the wine is reduced by half; strain and reserve. Melt butter in a saucepan, add flour and cook gently until it is pale straw-colored. Take from heat and stir in the stock, or clam juice and water, and wine. Season, bring to a boil, stirring, and simmer 2–3 minutes.

Mix the egg yolk with the cream, stir in a little of the hot sauce and slowly add this liaison to the remaining sauce. Reheat carefully until it thickens slightly but do not boil.

To prepare the garnish: peel cucumbers, cut in four lengthwise and trim into olive-shaped pieces with a vegetable peeler. Blanch in boiling water for 1 minute, drain and return to pan with butter and seasoning. Cook 3–4 minutes until tender, add dill, if used, and keep warm.

Let mold stand 4–5 minutes in a warm place, then turn out onto a hot platter. Spoon over sauce and garnish with hot cucumber.

Serve tomato fish mold with green peas and tomato sauce

Tomato Fish Mold

2 cans (6½ oz each) tuna in oil,
   or 2 cans (7¾ oz each) salmon
3 eggs, separated
½ cup heavy cream

For panada
5 tablespoons butter
6 tablespoons flour
1 tablespoon tomato paste
1½ cups chicken or veal stock,
   milk or water
salt and pepper

To serve
2 cups simple tomato sauce
2 cups cooked green peas or
   baby carrots

Ring mold (1½ quart capacity)

Method
To prepare the panada: melt the butter, stir in the flour with tomato paste and add stock, milk or water. Bring to a boil, stirring, cook 1–2 seconds, season well and spread on a plate to cool.

Butter the mold.

Flake tuna or salmon, removing any bones. Then pound fish in a mortar and pestle with any oil from can, and gradually work in cool panada. Or, instead of pounding, work flaked fish and oil with panada in a blender for a few seconds until mixture is just smooth. Beat in egg yolks and cream.

Beat egg whites until they hold a stiff peak and fold into fish mixture. Spoon into mold to within ¼ inch of the top, cover with foil and steam on top of the stove or cook in a water bath in a moderate oven (350°F) for 45–50 minutes or until firm to the touch.

Let stand 5 minutes in a warm place, then turn out onto a hot platter and coat with tomato sauce, serving the rest separately. Fill center with cooked peas or whole baby carrots, tossed in butter. If you like, use a mixture of both peas and carrots.

Fish Balls with Tomato Sauce

1½ lb fresh shad, rockfish or
   haddock fillet
2 cups fresh white breadcrumbs
1 egg white
salt and pepper
¼ cup white wine
½ cup water
1 tablespoon chopped parsley
2 cups simple tomato sauce

These fish balls, known as 'boulettes', are not cooked in a mold, but the mixture has a similar consistency and is made in the same way as the mixture for molds.

Method
Set oven at moderate (350°F).

Remove any skin and bones from fish, chop fish and pound in a mortar and pestle or work it in the blender. Soak breadcrumbs in cold water and squeeze dry in a piece of cheesecloth.

Work breadcrumbs into fish using a mortar and pestle or a blender, then work in egg white and seasoning. When mixture is very firm, shape into walnut-sized balls and set them in a buttered ovenproof baking dish. Pour over white wine and water, cover with foil and cook in heated oven for 15–20 minutes or until firm to the touch.

Transfer fish balls carefully to a hot serving dish, add chopped parsley to tomato sauce and spoon it over fish balls.

Fish Mold Newburg

1 lb haddock fillet
2 eggs, beaten to mix
6 tablespoons heavy cream

For panada
¼ cup butter
1 cup milk
6 tablespoons flour
salt and pepper

For sauce
2 tablespoons butter
½ tablespoon paprika
1½ tablespoons flour
1 cup fish stock or ½ cup
   clam juice and ½ cup water
   (mixed)
½ cup (¼ lb) cooked lobster
   meat or shrimps, coarsely
   chopped
2 tablespoons sherry
6 tablespoons heavy cream

*7 inch springform pan,
   kugelhopf or ring mold
   (1½ quart capacity)*

Method
To make the panada: melt the butter in the milk, bring just to a boil, take from heat, add the flour all at once and beat until mixture is smooth and pulls away from sides of pan. Season and cool.

Butter the pan or mold.

Remove any skin and bone from fish, chop flesh and pound until smooth in a mortar and pestle; gradually work in panada. Or, instead of pounding, work chopped fish and panada for a few seconds in a blender until just smooth. Beat in the eggs and cream and adjust seasoning.

Spoon the mixture into the prepared pan or mold to within ¼ inch of the top, cover with foil and steam on top of the stove or cook in a water bath in a moderate oven (350°F) for 40 minutes or until mold is firm to the touch.

To prepare the sauce: melt the butter, stir in paprika and cook gently for 1 minute. Stir in the flour and cook 1 minute longer or until the roux looks slightly separated. Take from heat, add stock, or clam juice and water, and bring to a boil, stirring; simmer 1–2 minutes.

Heat the lobster meat or shrimps in sherry over low heat for 2–3 minutes and add to sauce with cream. Taste for seasoning.

Let mold stand 5 minutes in a warm place, then turn out onto a hot platter and spoon over sauce.

Simple Tomato Sauce

1 can (1 lb) tomatoes
2 tablespoons butter
2 tablespoons flour
1½ teaspoons tomato paste
2 cups stock
salt and pepper
1 bay leaf
1 clove of garlic, crushed

Makes about 2 cups.

Method
Melt the butter in a pan, stir in the flour until smooth and cook until straw-colored. Blend in tomato paste and stock and stir until mixture boils.

Add tomatoes, crushing them well with the back of a wooden spoon, and stir in seasoning, bay leaf and garlic. Simmer 20–30 minutes, stirring occasionally, until the sauce is well reduced. Work the sauce through a strainer and use as required.

Ham Mold

2 cups (1 lb) ground lean
    cooked ham
thick béchamel sauce, made
    with $\frac{1}{4}$ cup butter, $\frac{1}{4}$ cup flour,
    $1\frac{1}{2}$ cups milk (infused with
    slice of onion, 6 peppercorns,
    blade of mace and bay leaf)
3 eggs
$\frac{1}{2}$ cup heavy cream
1 teaspoon Dijon-style or
    prepared mustard
salt and pepper

For parsley sauce
$1\frac{1}{2}$ cups parsley sprigs
2–3 scallions, cut in short
    lengths
3 tablespoons butter
3 tablespoons flour
2 cups milk

*6 inch springform pan or ring
   mold (5 cup capacity)*

Method
Butter pan or ring mold.
   Work ham twice through
the fine blade of the grinder.
Pound in a mortar and pestle
and work in cooled béchamel
sauce, beating well with a
wooden spoon. Or, instead of
pounding, mix ground ham
and sauce with electric mixer.
Beat in eggs, stir in cream and
season to taste with mustard
and a very little salt and
pepper.
   Spoon mixture into prepared mold or pan to within
$\frac{1}{4}$ inch of the top, cover with
foil and steam on top of the
stove or cook in a water bath
in a moderate oven (350°F)
for 60–65 minutes or until
firm to the touch.
   Meanwhile make parsley
sauce: cook parsley with
scallions in boiling salted
water for 7–8 minutes or until
tender. Drain well, press to
extract any water and work
through a sieve. Melt the
butter, stir in the flour and
pour in milk. Season and

bring the sauce to a boil,
stirring. Simmer 1–2 minutes
and add parsley purée. Or,
instead of sieving, the parsley
and scallion mixture can be
puréed in the blender with a
little of the sauce. Then add
to remaining sauce.
   Let mold stand 5 minutes
in a warm place, then turn out
onto a hot platter, coat with a
little of the sauce and serve
the rest separately.

Velouté Sauce

3 tablespoons butter
2 tablespoons flour
$2\frac{1}{4}$–$2\frac{1}{2}$ cups well-flavored veal
    or chicken stock
salt and pepper

Makes 2 cups.

Method
In a pan, melt the butter, stir
in the flour and cook until pale
straw-colored. Take from
heat, cool a little and pour in
the stock. Bring to a boil,

stirring, and simmer until the
sauce is glossy and coats the
back of a spoon. Season to
taste.

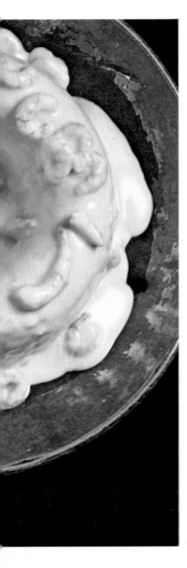

Veal mold (left) is coated with a velouté sauce with tomato strips and parsley added. Fish mold Newburg (right) is served with sherry-flavored sauce and cooked baby shrimps

Veal Mold

1 lb ground lean raw veal
1 tablespoon butter, melted
pinch of ground mace
3 eggs, beaten to mix
¼ cup heavy cream

For panada
5 tablespoons butter
5 tablespoons flour
1¼ cups milk
salt and pepper

For salpicon
2 small onions or shallots, finely chopped
3 tablespoons butter
1 cup (¼ lb) mushrooms, sliced
1½ tablespoons flour
½ cup stock
½ cup (¼ lb) shredded cooked ham or tongue

For sauce
2 cups velouté sauce
1–2 tablespoons heavy cream
squeeze of lemon juice
3 medium tomatoes, peeled, seeded and cut in strips
1 tablespoon chopped parsley

7 inch charlotte mold or 8 inch springform pan

For a variation of this dish, coat the mold with a plain velouté sauce (without tomatoes and parsley) and surround it with a garnish of cooked baby vegetables like new potatoes, carrots, peas and lima beans.

Method
To make the panada: melt the butter, stir in the flour, pour on the milk and bring to a boil, stirring. Cook 1–2 seconds, season and turn out onto a plate to cool.

Butter the mold or springform pan.

To prepare the salpicon: cook the onion or shallot in butter for 1–2 minutes until soft, add mushrooms and cook until tender. Take from heat and stir in flour, then pour in the stock. Bring to a boil, simmer 1–2 minutes and add ham or tongue, season and cool.

Pound veal in a mortar and pestle until smooth and gradually work in the panada. Or, instead of pounding, work veal and panada in a blender for a few seconds until just smooth. Beat in butter and mace and stir in eggs and add cream.

Transfer the mixture to the prepared mold or pan to within ¼ inch of the top; dip a spoon in water and hollow out the center. Spoon salpicon into this, carefully spread veal mixture over the top and smooth it. Cover with foil and steam on top of the stove or cook in a water bath in a moderate oven (350°F) for 45–50 minutes or until firm to the touch.

Meanwhile prepare velouté sauce. Take from heat and add cream. Stir in lemon juice, tomatoes and parsley and taste for seasoning.

Let mold stand 5 minutes in a warm place, then turn out onto a hot platter, spoon over enough sauce to coat it and serve the rest separately.

Add the tomato strips and chopped parsley to the velouté sauce for coating the veal mold

Chicken Molds

2½–3 lb chicken
3–4 slices of cooked tongue
⅓ cup butter, softened
salt and pepper
2 small eggs, beaten to mix
2 cups sauce Madère or demi-glace (for serving) – see page 90

For panada
¼ cup butter
1 cup milk
6 tablespoons flour

7–8 individual dariole molds or custard cups; 1½–2 inch plain cutter

Method
Cut flesh from the chicken, discarding the skin and bones; work it twice through fine blade of grinder. It should measure about 1½ cups.

To prepare panada: melt butter in the milk, bring just to a boil, take from heat, add the flour all at once and beat until mixture is smooth and pulls away from sides of pan. Spread on a plate to cool.

Set oven at moderate (350°F); butter molds or cups.

Cut out rounds of tongue to fit the bottom of the molds or cups; place in each one.

Pound chicken in a mortar and pestle until smooth, then gradually work in cool panada with butter. Or work ground chicken, panada and butter for a few seconds in blender until just smooth. Season well and stir in eggs.

Spoon the mixture into the prepared molds to within ¼ inch of the top, cover with foil and cook in a water bath in heated oven for 20–25 minutes or until firm.

Let molds stand 1–2 minutes in a warm place, turn out onto a hot platter and spoon around a little sauce, serving the rest separately.

Chicken Liver Mold

2–2½ lb chicken
1 cup (½ lb) chicken livers
⅓ cup butter, softened
salt and pepper
2 small eggs, beaten to mix
2 cups sauce Périgueux (for serving)

For panada
¼ cup butter
1 cup milk
6 tablespoons flour

Ring mold (5 cup capacity)

Method
Cut the flesh from the chicken, discarding the skin and bones, and work it twice through the fine blade of the grinder. It should measure about 1 cup. Work the liver through the grinder also.

To prepare the panada: melt the butter in the milk, bring just to a boil, take from the heat, add the flour all at once and beat thoroughly until the mixture is smooth and pulls away from the sides of the pan. Spread it on a plate to cool.

Set oven at moderate (350°F) and butter the mold.

Pound the chicken with the liver in a mortar and pestle until smooth or work the mixture until smooth in a blender. Work it through a sieve to remove any membrane from the liver. Return the mixture to the mortar and gradually work in the cool panada and the butter. If using a blender, work the chicken mixture, panada and butter together for a few seconds. Season well and stir in the eggs.

Spoon the mixture into the prepared mold to within ¼ inch of the top, cover with wax paper and place in a water bath. Bake in the heated oven for 45–50 minutes or until it is quite firm to the touch.

Let the mold stand 5 minutes in a warm place, then turn out onto a hot platter. Coat with a little sauce Périgueux and serve the rest separately.

Sauce Périgueux

2 cups sauce Madère
small can whole truffles or truffle pieces
2 tablespoons butter
salt and pepper
squeeze of lemon juice (optional)

Method
Drain the truffles, reserving the liquid, and if using whole ones, cut them in thin slices or julienne strips. Add the truffles and the liquid to the sauce Madère and simmer 5 minutes.

Take the sauce from the heat and whisk in the butter, a few pieces at a time. Taste the sauce for seasoning and add a little lemon juice, if you like.

Watchpoint: do not reheat the sauce or it may curdle.

Sauce Madère

½ cup Madeira
1 tablespoon tomato paste
4 cups espagnole sauce (see Volume 2)
½ cup well-flavored stock
2 tablespoons butter

Makes 4 cups.

Method
Stir tomato paste into the prepared espagnole sauce in a pan, simmer 5 minutes and add the stock. Continue to simmer, uncovered, skimming often, until well reduced.

Add the Madeira and beat in the butter in small pieces. Do not boil after this, but keep sauce warm or reheat in a water bath to serve.

Sauce Demi-glace

½ cup (2 oz) chopped mushrooms
1 tablespoon tomato paste
4 cups espagnole sauce (see Volume 2)
½ cup jellied stock
½ cup sherry
2 tablespoons butter

Makes 4 cups.

Method
Stir the mushrooms into the tomato paste and add both to the prepared espagnole sauce in a pan. Simmer 5 minutes, add the stock and continue to simmer uncovered, skimming often, until well reduced.

Add the sherry and beat in the butter. Do not boil after this, but keep sauce warm or reheat in a water bath to serve.

Suprême Sauce

2 cups velouté sauce (made with 3 tablespoons butter, 2 tablespoons flour, 2 cups well-flavored fish, chicken or veal stock, salt and pepper)
3–4 egg yolks
1 cup heavy cream

Makes 3 cups.

Method
Make velouté sauce (see method on page 88).

Mix the egg yolks with cream and stir in a little of the hot sauce. Stir this mixture gradually back into remaining sauce and heat until it thickens slightly; do not boil. Taste for seasoning.

Mousseline

This mixture resembles a mousse as it is lightly spongy rather than creamy in texture when cooked. Mousselines have a particularly delicate flavor; they can be made with fish, chicken, rabbit or veal and are used as a stuffing for fillets of sole or suprêmes (breasts) of chicken.

A mousseline mixture can also make a complete dish when shaped into dumplings called quenelles, or when cooked in individual molds and coated with an appropriate sauce.

Mousseline of Fish, Chicken Rabbit or Veal

1½ lb shad, pike, haddock or other firm fish, or raw chicken, or rabbit, or veal
3 egg whites, beaten until broken up
1½ cups heavy cream
salt and pepper
2–3 cups velouté (see page 88) or suprême sauce

Ring mold (1 quart capacity)

A variety of garnishes can be added to a sauce for mousselines; for a fish mousseline you can use ½ cup cooked, peeled chopped shrimps, and for fish or meat mousselines add ½ cup sliced mushrooms (cooked in a little butter and lemon juice) to the sauce.

Method
Butter the mold.

Remove any pieces of skin or bones, then pass fish or meat twice through the fine blade of the grinder; pound mixture in a mortar and pestle and gradually work in egg whites. Or, instead of pounding, work ground fish or meat and egg white for a few seconds in the blender until very smooth. Gradually beat in cream and then add seasoning.

Watchpoint: if the kitchen is hot, the mixture should be put in a metal bowl over a bowl of ice to chill it thoroughly while working in the cream. Do not season the mousseline until the egg whites and cream have been worked in — the consistency should be like whipped cream. If the mixture is at all soft, the addition of salt will stiffen it immediately.

Spoon the mousseline into prepared mold to within ¼ inch of the top, cover with foil and steam on top of the stove or cook in a water bath in a moderate oven (350°F) for 40–45 minutes or until firm to the touch.

Let stand 4–5 minutes in a warm place before turning out onto a hot platter, then coat with velouté or suprême sauce and serve remaining sauce separately.

Quenelles

These dumplings can be made with fish, chicken, rabbit, or veal; they are usually small and oval in shape and are poached in simmering salted water like eggs. Special quenelle molds are available and they must be thoroughly buttered before filling with the mixture. Alternatively, quenelles can be made without molds by using 2 tablespoons to shape them.

Make 1½ lb quantity mousseline mixture (with fish, chicken, rabbit or veal).

To Poach Quenelles
Use a large shallow pan. Fill prepared molds with mousse-

Fish quenelles are served with a velouté sauce, flavored with a little tomato paste, with shrimps and mushrooms added

line mixture level to the tops, and when the water is at boiling point, carefully lower molds so they sit on the bottom of the pan; the water should come 1½–2 inches above the molds and be kept barely at simmering point.

Shake pan gently from time to time; after about 7 minutes the quenelles will detach themselves from molds and rise to the surface. Lift them out carefully with a slotted spoon and drain on paper towels.

To serve, arrange quenelles in a hot dish and coat with velouté (see page 88), suprême or mushroom cream sauce.

To make Quenelles without Molds
Shape the mixture with 2 tablespoons and drop into the simmering water. Cook as above, turning them once, until firm to the touch. Drain and serve quenelles as above.

Mushroom Cream Sauce

To 2 cups velouté sauce: add 1 cup mushrooms, thinly sliced and cooked in a little butter and juice of ½ lemon for 1–2 minutes or until tender.

PRESERVES (3)

Just when some fruits become unobtainable, citrus fruits come triumphantly into season, brightening market displays with their colorful abundance. Citrus fruits make superb preserves — orange marmalade is an obvious favorite but lemon, lime and grapefruit marmalades and jellies are equally delicious. Unusual preserves like kumquats add interest to cold meats or a buffet table. This feature includes a recipe for dried apricots and for pineapple which are also available in winter.

The distinction between marmalades and jams is very small — marmalades generally contain pieces or slices of fruit suspended in a clear jelly, while jam is thicker and opaque. Both are made and tested in the same way, so look back to the detailed instructions on jam making in Preserves (1) in Volume 7.

Points to remember

1 Most of the work with citrus marmalades is slicing the fruit; if you do not have a mechanical slicer, you may prefer to try the first orange marmalade recipe where the fruit can be put through a grinder.

2 The preserve will be a better color and keep more of its fresh fruit flavor if it is cooked quickly in small batches, so it does not boil for too long.

3 When making marmalade, the peel must be tender before the sugar is added.

4 Carefully warm sugar in a low oven before adding to the boiling fruit so that the temperature of fruit is not lowered. The sugar then dissolves quickly and the fruit will not overcook.

5 When the sugar has dissolved, and not before, boil the mixture briskly, occasionally stirring gently but slowly until the preserve gives a jell test.

6 In general, marmalades and spiced preserves should be sealed when still hot. However, if the preserve contains large pieces of fruit, these may float to the top on standing, so the mixture must be partly cooled, then thoroughly stirred before packing into clean, dry jars or glasses. Jams and jellies are usually sealed when cool.

7 When correctly made, sealed and stored, marmalades, jams and jellies can be kept for 6–8 months in a cool dry place. The flavor of spiced preserves mellows on keeping; they should be used within 3–4 months or within a month if covered but not sealed.

To Test for Jell Point

Draw preserving kettle aside, quickly cool a little fruit mixture on a cold plate (or drop a little on the bottom of an ice cube tray taken straight from freezer). Run your index finger through center and if the preserve is ready it will crinkle slightly and remain in 2 separate portions. It will also form a firm drop on the finger.

You can also test with a sugar thermometer. Warm the thermometer in hot water, then stir the jam thoroughly to make the temperature even throughout and dip thermometer well into the mixture. When the temperature reaches 220°F, the jell is right.

To Skim and Store

Preserves may need skimming to remove any scum from the top. Do this only towards the end of cooking as continuous skimming is unnecessary and wasteful.

Jars or glasses for preserves must be sterilized and dry. Warm them in a very low oven before filling, stand on a wooden board to prevent cracking and fill them completely full to allow for shrinkage. Then carefully wipe the outside of the filled jars or glasses with a cloth wrung out in hot water. Cover with a thin layer of melted paraffin.

When the paraffin solidifies, add a second layer and cover the jars or glasses with lids or circles of white or wax paper or plastic wrap fastened with elastic bands or string. Label each jar or glass with the name of the preserves and the date. Store in a cool, dry place.

Orange Marmalade 1

4 bitter, Seville or sour oranges
2 sweet oranges
1 lemon
2½ quarts water
8 cups sugar

This marmalade is smoother than orange marmalade 2.

Method

Cut the oranges and lemon in half, squeeze out the juice, strain it and wrap the fruit seeds in a piece of cheesecloth tied with a long piece of string. Cut the peel and pulp into fine slices or work through the coarse blade of the grinder. Put in a large bowl (not aluminum) with the water, juice and bag of seeds, cover and let soak for 24 hours.

Transfer the mixture to a preserving kettle and tie the string on the cheesecloth bag to the pan handle for easy removal. Bring to a boil and cook steadily until the mixture is reduced by half — this will take about 1 hour. Warm the sugar in a low oven (250°F).

Squeeze liquid and pectin from the cheesecloth bag by pressing against the side of the kettle; discard the bag. Add the warmed sugar, heat gently, stirring until all the sugar has dissolved, then bring to a boil and cook rapidly for about 30 minutes until the marmalade gives a jell test. Towards the end of cooking, stir frequently.

Take from heat, skim marmalade well, then pour into hot, dry jars and seal at once.

Note: if you have not made jam or jelly before, refer to the general rules for preserving given in Volume 7.

Orange Marmalade 2

3 bitter, Seville or sour oranges
1 large sweet orange
1 lemon
5 cups sugar
1 quart water

Method

Boil the fruit whole in water to cover for 1½ hours or until soft; drain. Peel oranges and lemon very thinly and cut rind in fine slices. Cut pith from flesh with a serrated-edge knife and reserve. Slice flesh in horizontal one-eighth inch slices, remove seeds and reserve. Tie pith and seeds in a piece of cheesecloth.

Put the sliced fruit and rind in a large bowl (not aluminum) with the sugar, 1 quart water, and cheesecloth bag. Cover and let stand overnight.

Transfer to a preserving kettle, heat gently, stirring until all the sugar has dissolved, then bring to a boil and cook rapidly until marmalade gives a jell test. Squeeze liquid and pectin from cheesecloth bag by pressing against the side of the kettle; discard bag.

Take from heat, skim marmalade well, then pour into hot, dry jars and seal at once.

If substituting **regular oranges** for **Seville oranges** in a recipe, decrease the quantity of sugar by one-third cup per orange. The sour, bitter pulp of Seville oranges makes extra sugar necessary in cooking.

A selection of home-made preserves is a welcome addition to a store cupboard

Three Fruit Marmalade

2 grapefruits
2 sweet oranges
2 lemons
water
sugar

Method

Choose thin-skinned fruit. Quarter the fruit and slice it very thinly, reserving the seeds. Measure the fruit with its juice and add three times the quantity of water in a large bowl (not aluminum). Tie seeds in a piece of cheesecloth, add to fruit, cover and let soak for 24 hours.

Then squeeze liquid and pectin from cheesecloth bag by pressing against side of bowl; discard bag.

Transfer fruit to a preserving kettle and boil for $\frac{3}{4}$ hour or until liquid is reduced by half. Measure amount of fruit again and add an equal amount of sugar (from sugar previously warmed in a low oven at 250°F). Heat gently, stirring until all sugar has dissolved, then bring to a boil and cook rapidly until marmalade gives a jell test.

Take from heat, skim marmalade well and let stand 30 minutes. Stir well to distribute pieces of fruit evenly, pour into hot, dry jars and seal at once.

Tangerine Marmalade

9 tangerines
3 lemons
1$\frac{1}{2}$ quarts water
7 cups sugar

Method

Peel lemons very thinly; cut pith from flesh with a serrated-edge knife and reserve both rind and pith.

Cut lemons and tangerines in half and squeeze out juice. Remove the central membranes from tangerine peel and put in a small bowl with seeds, lemon pith and 1 cup of the water. Shred tangerine peel and the strips of lemon rind.

Put fruit juices, shredded peel and rind and remaining water in a large bowl (not aluminum), cover and leave overnight. Transfer to a preserving kettle, add membranes, pith and seeds, tied in a piece of cheesecloth, and the water in which they have been soaking. Boil steadily for $\frac{1}{2}$ hour or until fruit peel is tender. Heat sugar in a low oven (250°F).

Squeeze the liquid and pectin from the cheesecloth bag by pressing against the side of the kettle; discard the bag. Add warmed sugar to the pan, heat gently, stirring until all the sugar has dissolved; bring to a boil and cook rapidly until the marmalade gives a jell test.

Take from heat, skim marmalade well, pour into hot, dry jars and seal at once.

95

Pineapple and Grapefruit Marmalade

1 pineapple
1 grapefruit
1 lemon
water
sugar

Method

Peel and core pineapple and cut flesh in thin slices. Chop the slices coarsely. Thinly slice grapefruit and lemon and discard any pips. Combine the fruit in a large bowl (not aluminum), measure it and add 3 cups water to every cup of fruit. Cover and let stand overnight.

Put the fruit mixture in a pan, cover and boil 20 minutes or until the fruit peel is very tender. Let stand again overnight.

Measure the fruit and juice and warm an equal amount of sugar in a low oven (250°F). Transfer fruit and juice to a preserving kettle and bring to a boil. Add the warm sugar, heat gently, stirring until all the sugar has dissolved, then bring to a boil and cook rapidly until marmalade gives a jell test.

Take from heat, skim marmalade well and let stand 30 minutes. Stir well to distribute fruit evenly. Pour into hot, dry jars and seal at once.

Pineapple Jam

1 large pineapple
3 cups sugar
grated rind and juice of
   3 lemons
1 cup golden raisins

Method

Peel and cut the pineapple and dice the flesh.

Heat the sugar in a low oven (250°F).

Put the pineapple with the lemon rind and juice in a preserving kettle and bring to a boil. Add the sugar and heat gently, stirring, until the sugar is dissolved. Bring back to a boil and cook rapidly for 30 minutes or until the jam gives a jell test. Add the raisins and cook 1 minute longer.

Skim the jam well, pour into hot, dry glasses and seal at once.

Pectin is a natural, gum-like substance which causes preserves to jell. It is present to some extent in most fruit; all citrus fruits have a high pectin content, so do tart apples, plums, currants and gooseberries, particularly when they are slightly underripe.

Green Grape Jam

4 cups (2 lb) seedless green
   grapes
1 cup water
4 cups sugar
juice of 1 lemon

Method

Wash the grapes and discard the stems. Put them in a preserving kettle with the water, bring to a boil, cover and simmer until the grapes are tender.

Heat the sugar in a low oven (250°F). Add to the grapes with the lemon juice. Heat gently, stirring, until the sugar is dissolved. Bring to a boil and cook rapidly until the jam gives a jell test.

Take from the heat, skim the jam well and let cool 15–20 minutes. Stir to mix the fruit and syrup thoroughly and pour into hot, dry glasses. Seal at once.

Rhubarb and Ginger Jam

3 lb rhubarb (weighed after
   removing leaf and bottom of
   stalk)
$\frac{1}{4}$ cup finely chopped candied
   ginger
1 large tart apple
4 cups sugar
$\frac{1}{4}$ cup chopped mixed candied
   peel
grated rind and strained
   juice of $\frac{1}{2}$ lemon

Method

Wipe rhubarb, cut it in pieces; pare, core and slice apple. Layer rhubarb and apple with sugar in a large bowl (not aluminum), cover and let stand overnight.

Transfer to a preserving kettle, add candied peel and ginger with grated lemon rind and juice. Heat gently, stirring until all the sugar has dissolved, then bring slowly to a boil and cook rapidly until jam gives a jell test.

Take from heat, skim well and pour jam into hot, dry jars; seal when cool.

Note: if you have not made jam or jelly before, refer to the general rules for preserving given in Volume 7.

Dried Apricot Jam

4½ cups (1½ lb) dried apricots
2½ quarts water
8 cups sugar

If possible, use deeply colored, dried apricots for this unusual jam as they have a better flavor than pale, sweet ones.

Method
Put apricots in a large bowl (not aluminum), add the water and soak for 36 hours. Transfer apricots and water to a preserving kettle, and bring slowly to a boil. Heat sugar in a low oven (250°F) and add to the fruit. Heat gently, stirring until the sugar has dissolved, bring to a boil and cook rapidly until the jam gives a jell test.

Take from heat, skim the jam well, then pour into hot, dry jars and seal when cool.

Kumquat or Calamondin Preserves

3 lb kumquats or calamondins
water
sugar

Method
Cut the fruit in half and scoop out the flesh, reserving it. Cover the peel with cold water, bring to a boil and simmer 20 minutes or until tender, changing the water 2–3 times to avoid a bitter flavor. Drain and shred the peel.

Meanwhile combine the flesh with 3 cups water in a pan, cover and simmer 30 minutes. Strain, discarding the flesh, and add 3 more cups water to the juice. Measure the juice and to each

cup of juice allow ¾ cup sugar. Heat the sugar in a low oven (250°F).

Put the juice in a preserving kettle, bring to a boil, add the warmed sugar and heat gently, stirring until all the sugar has dissolved. Add shredded peel, bring to a boil and cook rapidly until the preserves give a jell test.

Take from heat, skim well and pour preserves into hot, dry jars. Seal at once.

Orange Lemon Jelly

6 oranges
juice of 6 lemons
water
sugar

Method
Measure lemon juice in a large bowl (not aluminum) and add three times as much water. Cut oranges, including rind, in slices and add to lemon juice and water. Cover and let stand overnight.

Transfer the mixture to a pan, bring to a boil, cover and simmer 1 hour or until liquid is reduced by half. Strain through a jelly bag or several layers of cheesecloth, letting the liquid drip through slowly — do not squeeze or the jelly will be cloudy.

Measure juice and allow 1¾ cups sugar to each 2 cups juice. Heat sugar in a low oven (250°F).

Transfer the juice to a preserving kettle and bring to a boil. Stir in the warmed sugar and heat gently, stirring until all the sugar has dissolved. Bring to a boil and cook rapidly until the jelly gives a jell test. Take from heat, skim well and pour jelly into hot, dry jars. Seal when cool.

Spiced Tangerines

8 unblemished tangerines
4 cups sugar
4 cups water
1 cup white wine vinegar
12 cloves
3-inch piece of cinnamon

Method
Simmer tangerines in water to cover for 1½ hours or until they can be pierced easily with a skewer. Drain them and prick them all over with a skewer.

Combine the sugar, 4 cups water and vinegar and bring to a boil, add the tangerines and spices, tied in a cheesecloth bag, cover and simmer 30 minutes. Lift out tangerines, cut in half if you like and pack into 1-quart jars. Discard the cheesecloth bag; pour over the hot syrup and seal at once.

Lime Jelly

10 limes
5 cups water
sugar

Method
Slice limes thinly, put them in a bowl (not aluminum) with the water, cover and let stand overnight.

Put the fruit in a pan, bring to a boil, cover and simmer 1 hour or until the limes are very tender. Strain juice through a jelly bag or through several layers of cheesecloth letting the liquid drip through slowly — do not squeeze or the jelly will be cloudy. Measure the juice and allow ¾ cup sugar for each cup of juice. Heat the sugar in a low oven (250°F).

Put the juice in a preserving kettle, bring to a boil, add the warmed sugar and heat gently, stirring, until the sugar has dissolved. Bring to a boil and cook rapidly until it gives a jell test.

Take from heat, skim jelly well, then pour into hot, dry jars and seal when cool.

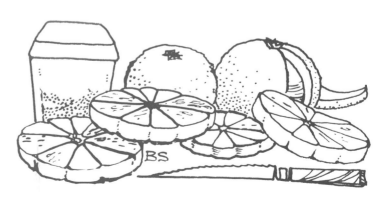

HOMEMADE VINEGARS

Vinegar, like wine, is made by a natural process. Fruit juice or any liquid containing sugar will turn into alcohol if brought into contact with yeast at the right temperature. Grape juice makes the best wine and yeast (a microscopic plant) does not have to be added as it is present in the 'bloom' on the grape skins.

If exposed to air, the alcohol in wine is worked on by bacteria to make acetic acid. The result is 'vin aigre (sour wine) vinegar. Wine vinegar made from grapes has the finest flavor. All kinds of vinegar can be flavored with herbs, flowers, spices or vegetables and then they have various uses: some are added to marinades and sauces; strong vinegars are invaluable for pickles, while mild vinegars are best for dressings.

Fruit or flower-flavored vinegars even make a refreshing drink when sugar is added.

KINDS OF VINEGARS

Wine vinegar may be red or white. White wine vinegar is used for salad dressings, for light-colored vegetables, aspics, court bouillon, and hollandaise sauce, pickles and relishes. Red wine vinegar is used for marinades and dressings or to add piquancy to stews and sauces.

Cider vinegar is made from fermented apple juice and is a good substitute for white wine vinegar because its flavor is mild.

Distilled vinegar is the basis of most herb vinegars and is used for pickles, relishes and preserves but for many dressings its flavor is too harsh.

Herb vinegars — tarragon, mint, garlic and dill for instance — are made by steeping the herbs in distilled or wine vinegar for a minimum of three months.

Malt vinegar is available at some specialty stores. It is a vinegar made from sour ale or beer and is used throughout Europe.

Tarragon Vinegar

Take 2 large bunches of fresh tarragon and bruise the leaves and the tender part of the stalks. Pack them into a $1\frac{1}{2}$–2 quart jar and fill the jar with white wine vinegar. Cover tightly and leave 6–8 weeks.

Put 2–3 sprigs of soaked tarragon in three 16 oz bottles and strain in the vinegar. Screw tightly. Vinegar should be stored in a cool, dark place.

Fresh rosemary, basil, dill, thyme, savory and oregano can all be substituted for tarragon in this recipe.

Mint Vinegar

Strip the leaves from the stalks of 2 large bunches of mint. Wash and dry them thoroughly. Pack the leaves into a $1\frac{1}{2}$–2 quart jar and cover with red or white vinegar — this will take about 6 cups. Cover tightly and leave 3–4 weeks.

Strain the vinegar into three 16 oz bottles, discarding the mint, and screw tightly.

Summer Vinegar

Pack 2–3 cups of nasturtium flowers (use dry flowers that are not bruised) into a $1\frac{1}{2}$–2 quart jar and press down well. Add a large pinch of salt and $\frac{1}{2}$ teaspoon of cayenne. Pour in 5 cups white wine vinegar and cover tightly.

After 2 days, add a little more vinegar to the jar and leave for at least 10 days. Strain into three 16 oz bottles.

This vinegar is good with fish.

Raspberry Vinegar

Lightly crush $1\frac{1}{2}$ lb raspberries and put them in a bowl with 2 cups white distilled vinegar. Cover and let stand for 1 week; stir every day.

Strain the vinegar through a jelly cloth or cheesecloth and measure the juice. Add 1 cup granulated sugar for every $1\frac{1}{2}$ cups of juice.

In a saucepan stir the mixture over low heat until the sugar is dissolved, bring to a boil and cook rapidly for 15 minutes, skimming well. Cool, pour the vinegar into bottles, and cover tightly.

Use this vinegar for dressing fruit salads.

For a refreshing drink, add 2–3 tablespoons of raspberry vinegar to a glass of club soda water.

Cucumber Vinegar

Into a pan put 8 small cucumbers, peeled and coarsely chopped. Add 2 onions, finely chopped, 1 tablespoon salt, and a dash of Tabasco or pinch of cayenne. Cover with white wine or distilled vinegar (5–6 cups). Bring to a boil, cook rapidly for 3 minutes and pour into a large crock or bowl. Cover tightly and leave for 1 week.

Strain the vinegar into three 16 oz bottles, add a piece of fresh dill to each bottle, if you like, and cover tightly.

Use this vinegar for dressings for fish and cucumber salads.

Celery Vinegar

Into a large crock or jar put 1 bunch of celery, thinly sliced, with 1 tablespoon celery seed. In a pan heat 6 cups of white wine vinegar with 1 tablespoon sugar until the sugar is dissolved; bring to a boil and pour over the celery. Cool, cover tightly and leave 2–3 weeks. Strain the vinegar into three 16 oz bottles and cover tightly.

Use in pickles and dressings for potatoes and other root vegetables.

Note: keep vinegar away from metal pans or metal lids of jars as it will take on an unpleasant metallic flavor.

Rose Petal Vinegar

Pick over 3 cups dark red rose petals carefully to make sure there are no bruised ones. Replace any petals you discard and pack them firmly into the measuring cup to make sure you have enough. Place them in a large jar.

In a pan heat gently 3 cups of white distilled vinegar with 5 tablespoons sugar until the sugar is dissolved; cool.

Pour the vinegar and sugar over the rose petals in the jar and leave, tightly covered, for 3–4 weeks. Strain into two 16 oz bottles and cover tightly.

This vinegar gives a pleasant flavor of roses to fruit salad.

Horseradish Vinegar

Wash and peel a 4-inch piece of horseradish root and grate it coarsely. Pack the grated horseradish into two 16 oz bottles. Add 1 teaspoon salt, $\frac{1}{2}$ teaspoon sugar and a small piece of fresh chili to each jar. Fill to the top with white or spiced vinegar. Cover tightly.

Strain the vinegar and press the horseradish lightly to remove excess liquid.

Use this vinegar for sauces, sprinkled over beet salad, or for salad dressing.

Chili Vinegar

Split in half 10–12 red or green chilies and remove the seeds.

Watchpoint: be careful when handling hot chilies as the oils in their flesh can make your eyes burn. Wear rubber gloves if handling fresh ones.

In a saucepan bring to a boil 6 cups white distilled vinegar, add the chilies and bring back to a boil. Pour into a large jar and leave, covered tightly, for 5–6 weeks.

Strain the vinegar into three 16 oz jars and cover tightly.

If using red chilies, leave for a week longer or the flavor will not be as strong.

Spiced Vinegar

Pound or crush $\frac{1}{4}$ cup black peppercorns with 2 tablespoons dried ginger root, cut in pieces, and 1 tablespoon allspice berries. Put them in a large heatproof jar. Add 6 cups of white distilled vinegar, 1 tablespoon salt, 4 shallots, finely chopped, 2 cloves of garlic, crushed, and 2 bay leaves. Cover tightly and let stand in a warm place for 1 week. Then place in a water bath, loosen the lid of the jar and poach for 1 hour.

Let cool, then strain the vinegar into three 16 oz jars and cover tightly.

Shallot Vinegar

Put into a large jar 1 pint box of shallots, chopped, and 6 cups white distilled vinegar. Cover tightly and leave for 10 days, shaking the jar at least once every day.

Strain the vinegar into three 16 oz jars and cover tightly.

Tomato Vinegar

Take 3 lb ripe tomatoes and cut each tomato into wedges, leaving the wedges attached at the bottom. Layer them with salt in a deep baking dish or casserole, cover tightly and bake in a very low oven (200°F) for 6–8 hours or overnight. Transfer the tomatoes and juice to a large jar.

In a pan bring to a boil 4 cups distilled white vinegar with $\frac{1}{4}$ cup of mustard seeds, $\frac{1}{4}$ teaspoon each of ground mace, cloves and nutmeg and 2 tablespoons salt. Pour vinegar mixture over the tomatoes and cover tightly. Let stand 5–7 days, shaking the jar several times a day.

Strain the vinegar into three or four 16 oz jars and cover tightly.

101

An elegant dinner begins with Turkish yogurt soup, followed by ballotine of chicken with prunes and a rich praline cream for dessert (recipes are on pages 106–107)

MENUS FOR MANY

Take your choice of three varied menus for 12 people — each menu designed for a different occasion. An elegant dinner with a touch of the exotic begins with Turkish yogurt soup, followed by a chicken ballotine stuffed with prunes, and a rich praline cream for dessert.

If you are planning a lavish cold luncheon, consider a menu of chilled curry-flavored soup, followed by vitello tonnato — a classic dish of veal in a tuna sauce — and a refreshing tangerine mousse for dessert. Or, for a splendidly simple cold buffet, serve steak flan in aspic, then fresh strawberries Cardinal.

These menus call for wines that can be purchased in quantity and served with both first and second courses — see individual menus for suggestions.

MENU 1

Potage Pondicherry
(Cream of Leek & Rice Soup)

Vitello Tonnato
(Boned Veal with Tuna Sauce)

Tangerine Mousse

∽∾

White wine — Verdicchio (Italy)
or Dry Semillon (California)

MENU 2

Cacik
(Turkish Yogurt Soup)

Ballotines of Chicken
with Prunes

Currant & Pistachio Pilaf

Praline Cream

∽∾

White wine — Vouvray (Loire)
or Elvira (New York)

MENU 3

Steak Flan

Zucchini Salad

Strawberries Cardinal

∽∾

Red wine — Bardolino (Italy)
or Grignolino (California)

Menu 1

Appetizer

Entrée

and a little salt, if necessary.

Arrange the veal slices, overlapping, on a platter and spoon over the sauce to coat them. Let the veal stand in a cool place or in the refrigerator for 24 hours to absorb the flavors of the sauce.

Just before serving, garnish with lemon slices and serve with a green salad.

<table>
<tr><td>

TIMETABLE

Day before
Cook veal and cool it; make tuna sauce.
Thinly slice veal, arrange on a platter, coat with sauce and keep in cool place or in refrigerator.
Wash greens for salad and store in a plastic bag in refrigerator. Make vinaigrette dressing.
Make chocolate squares or chop walnuts to decorate tangerine mousse.

Morning
Make soup, add liaison and chill; chop chives for garnish.
Slice lemon for veal garnish.
Make tangerine mousse, cover tightly and keep in refrigerator.

Before serving
Pour soup into bowls, top with chives and keep in refrigerator.
Stiffly whip cream and decorate mousse.
Garnish veal with lemon slices.
Toss salad with dressing; serve at once.

</td></tr>
</table>

Potage Pondicherry (Cream of Leek and Rice Soup)

7–8 small leeks, trimmed
$\frac{1}{2}$ cup long grain rice
$\frac{1}{4}$ cup butter
2 teaspoons curry powder
8 cups veal or chicken stock
1 cup light cream
salt
black pepper, freshly ground
2 tablespoons chopped chives (for garnish)

For liaison
1 egg yolk
5–6 tablespoons light cream

Method
Wash the leeks thoroughly and cut them in slices.

Melt the butter in a kettle, add the leeks, cover and cook over a very low heat until almost tender. Remove from the heat and stir in the curry powder. Cook gently for 1–2 minutes, then add the rice and stock, bring to a boil, cover and cook over a low heat for 30–40 minutes or until rice is very tender. Add the cream, season with salt and pepper and work through a sieve or in a blender.

Return the soup to the kettle. Mix the egg yolk with the cream, stir in a little hot soup and add this to the remaining soup; reheat gently until the mixture thickens slightly but do not boil. Serve chilled and sprinkle with chopped chives.

Vitello Tonnato (Veal with Tuna Sauce)

5 lb boned leg of veal, rolled and tied
1 onion stuck with 4 cloves
2 stalks of celery
2 carrots, quartered
bouquet garni
1 teaspoon salt

For tuna sauce
2 cans ($6\frac{1}{2}$ oz each) tuna in oil, flaked
small can of anchovy fillets, chopped
1 cup olive oil
2 tablespoons capers, drained
juice of 1–2 lemons or $\frac{1}{4}$–$\frac{1}{2}$ cup white wine
salt and pepper
1 lemon, thinly sliced (for garnish)

Method
In a kettle put the veal with the onion, celery, carrots, bouquet garni, salt and water to cover. Add the lid and simmer 2–$2\frac{1}{2}$ hours or until the veal is very tender when pierced with a skewer. Let cool in the liquid, then drain, remove the strings and carve in very thin slices; strain and reserve the cooking liquid.

To make tuna sauce: pound the tuna and anchovy fillets in a mortar and pestle, then gradually work in the olive oil to make a smooth thick sauce. Alternatively, work the tuna and anchovies, a little at a time, with some of the oil in a blender, then beat in the remaining oil. Stir in the capers with lemon juice or white wine to taste and thin with reserved cooking liquid to a consistency to coat the back of a spoon. Add pepper

---

Dessert

Tangerine Mousse

grated rind and juice of 5–6 tangerines (to give $1\frac{1}{2}$ cups juice)
6 eggs
4 egg yolks
$\frac{1}{2}$ cup sugar
2 envelopes gelatin
juice of 2 lemons, strained
1 cup heavy cream, whipped until it holds a soft shape

For decoration
1 cup heavy cream, stiffly whipped
chocolate squares (see box) or $\frac{1}{2}$ cup walnuts, chopped

2 soufflé dishes or bowls (1$\frac{1}{2}$ quart capacity each); pastry bag and medium star tube

Method
Put the eggs, egg yolks and sugar in a bowl and beat until mixed. Set the bowl over a pan of hot but not boiling water and beat until the mixture is thick and light and leaves a ribbon trail on itself when the beater is lifted. Take from heat and beat until cool. If using an electric beater, no heat is necessary.

Tangerine mousse is a decorative dessert

Sprinkle the gelatin over the lemon juice and let stand 5 minutes or until spongy. Dissolve gelatin over a pan of hot water and stir into the egg mixture with the tangerine juice and grated rind. Chill bowl over a pan of ice water, stirring gently until mixture is on the point of setting.

Fold in the lightly whipped cream and pour at once into the prepared molds; cover and chill at least 2 hours or until set.

Shortly before serving, put the stiffly whipped cream into the pastry bag fitted with the star tube and cover the top of the mousse with rosettes. Decorate with chocolate squares or chopped walnuts and serve.

To Make Chocolate Squares

For 16 squares: grate or finely chop 3 squares (3 oz) semisweet chocolate and melt on a heatproof plate over a pan of hot water, working with a metal spatula until the chocolate is smooth; do not heat it above tepid.

Spread chocolate thinly and evenly (about one-eighth inch thick) on an 8 inch wax paper or foil square and, when almost hard, mark into 2 inch squares with a sharp knife. Refrigerate until hard, then peel away paper/foil.

Menu 2

Appetizer

Entrée

TIMETABLE

Day before
Prepare and roll ballotines; make stock. If made ahead and frozen, take packages from freezer.
Make praline.
Blanch pistachios for pilaf.

Morning
Make yogurt soup and chill; chop chives for garnish.
Cook ballotines and keep in refrigerator.
Make sauce; cook garnish (if not done) and keep in refrigerator. Cook pilaf.
Make praline creams; prepare pineapple and keep tightly covered in refrigerator.

Shortly before serving
Set oven at moderately low (325°F). Put pilaf and ballotines in oven to reheat for 30–40 minutes.
Unmold praline creams, add pineapple and keep in refrigerator.
Spoon soup into bowls, add garnish and keep refrigerated.

Just before serving
Reheat ballotine garnish and sauce on top of stove.
Slice ballotines, arrange on a platter with garnish and serve sauce and pilaf separately.

Cacik
(Yogurt soup)

6 cups plain yogurt
3 medium cucumbers, peeled
4 cloves of garlic, crushed
3 tablespoons chopped fresh mint
salt and white pepper

This soup is served as a refreshing appetizer in Turkey. If possible, use tart goats' milk yogurt or, when this is unobtainable, sharpen the soup by adding 3 tablespoons of white vinegar. This recipe was first given in Volume 12.

Method
Cut the cucumbers in half lengthwise, scoop out the seeds with a teaspoon, and grate the cucumber flesh. Pile it in a colander, sprinkle it with a little salt and let stand 30 minutes to draw out the juices (dégorger).

Mix the garlic (adjust quantities to your taste) with a little of the yogurt. Stir this into the remaining yogurt with the grated cucumber, half the mint and salt and white pepper to taste.

Cover the soup and chill thoroughly. Serve in bowls sprinkled with the remaining chopped mint.

Ballotines of Chicken with Prunes

2 roasting chickens (4–4½ lb each)
1½ lb pitted prunes, soaked overnight in freshly brewed tea and drained
1½ cups red wine or port
4½–5 cups chicken stock (made with bones and giblets from chicken)
2 tablespoons butter

For stuffing
¼ cup butter
2 large onions, finely chopped
2 lb ground pork
2 teaspoons dried sage
2 tablespoons chopped parsley
3 cups fresh white breadcrumbs
salt and pepper
2 eggs, beaten to mix

For garnish
2–3 dozen small onions, blanched and peeled
6 tablespoons butter
1 tablespoon sugar
4 cups (1 lb) small mushrooms

For sauce
¼ cup butter
3 tablespoons flour
well-flavored chicken stock
1 tablespoon tomato paste
bouquet garni

This dish can be partly prepared ahead and frozen.

Method
Simmer the prunes in the wine or port for 10–15 minutes or until tender; let cool. Drain the liquid and reserve it to use in the sauce.

Bone the chickens (see detailed instructions in Volume 1) and make the stock.

To prepare the stuffing:

melt the butter, add the chopped onion and cook until soft but not brown. Let cool, then mix with the ground pork, herbs, breadcrumbs and plenty of seasoning. Bind the mixture with the beaten eggs.

Spread the stuffing on the chickens, arrange a line of prunes down the center and roll each chicken up tightly and neatly. Sew them, then tie in several places to make a roll.

To freeze: wrap the ballotines in foil and a plastic bag. Also strain and freeze the stock.

To make the garnish: put the onions in a saucepan with ¼ cup butter and the sugar. Cover and cook, shaking the pan frequently, until onions are tender and brown with caramelized sugar. Wipe the mushrooms with a damp cloth and sauté them in the remaining butter. Combine onions, mushrooms and remaining prunes. If you like, pack this garnish into a container for freezing.

To make the sauce: melt the butter, stir in the flour and cook slowly to a rich brown. Stir in 4 cups stock, tomato paste and bouquet garni and continue stirring until the mixture boils. Add salt and pepper to taste and simmer 15–20 minutes. Remove bouquet garni, skim the sauce well, add reserved cooking liquid from prunes and continue simmering for about 10 minutes; taste for seasoning. If freezing, let stand until cold before packing into containers.

To cook the chickens: if the ballotines have been frozen, let stand in the refrigerator for about 12 hours to thaw. Brown the ballotines on all sides in 2 tablespoons butter. Pour over about ½ cup well-flavored stock, cover tightly and cook for about 1½ hours or until a skewer inserted in

How To Bone A Chicken

1 Remove the trussing string or skewer. With a sharp knife, slit the skin along the backbone. Work skin and flesh from this area of carcass with the small knife until leg joint is reached, sever it.

2 Hold the end of the ball joint firmly in one hand. Cut away flesh with knife and scrape the thigh bone completely clean, always working from the inside of the leg. Clean drumstick until the whole leg bone is free of flesh

3 Sever the wing joint from carcass, leaving the bone attached to chicken meat. Still using knife, separate white meat from breastbone, leaving carcass intact; stop there. Now free the other wing and breast

4 Carefully cut away the skin from the top of the breastbone without splitting skin; keep both sides of bird attached so that it remains in one piece for stuffing

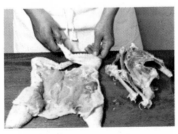

5 Lay the chicken flat ready for the stuffing to spread over the cut surfaces. Then sew up or secure with poultry pins and string; it is now ready to stuff

the center for 1 minute is hot to the touch when withdrawn. If the pan gets dry during cooking, add a little more stock.

To serve, slice the ballotines, arrange the slices overlapping on a platter, spoon over a little of the sauce and garnish with the reheated mixture of prunes, onions, and mushrooms.

Serve with pilaf of currants and pistachios (recipe is included in Volume 12).

Dessert

Praline Cream

1 cup whole, unblanched almonds
2 cups heavy cream
1 cup sugar

For cream
4 cups milk
8 egg yolks
$\frac{1}{3}$ cup sugar
2 envelopes gelatin
$\frac{1}{2}$ cup cold water

To finish
2 fresh pineapples or 2 cans (14 oz each) pineapple slices
$\frac{1}{2}$ cup sugar (for fresh pineapple)
$\frac{1}{4}$ cup kirsch (optional)

2 fluted ring molds (5 cup capacity each)

Method
Lightly oil the molds and a baking sheet.

To prepare the praline: put the almonds and sugar in a heavy-based pan. Cook over a low heat until the sugar melts, shaking the pan occasionally. When the sugar turns a pale golden brown, stir the mixture with a metal spoon and continue cooking until it is dark brown; do not let it burn. Pour at once onto the oiled baking sheet and leave until cold and hard.

Grind praline in a rotary cheese grater or in a grinder or work in a blender a little at a time, and reserve.

To make the cream: sprinkle the gelatin over the water in a bowl and let stand 5 minutes or until spongy. Scald the milk; beat the egg yolks and sugar together until thick and light, then gradually pour in the hot milk. Return the mixture to the pan and cook over a low heat, stirring constantly,

until the custard coats the back of a wooden spoon.
Watchpoint: do not let the custard boil or it will curdle.

Stir the gelatin into the custard until dissolved, strain into a bowl and let stand until cool. Whip the cream until it holds a soft shape.

Stand the bowl of custard over a bowl of ice water, add the praline and stir gently until it begins to thicken. Fold in the lightly whipped cream and pour the mixture into the prepared molds. Cover tightly with plastic wrap and refrigerate until firm.

Cut the skin from the fresh pineapples and slice the flesh, discarding the cores. Sprinkle the slices with sugar and then with kirsch, if you like. Alternatively, drain canned pineapple and sprinkle with kirsch.

Just before serving, unmold the praline creams onto a platter and garnish the center and sides with the pineapple slices.

For steak flan, the baked pastry shells are filled with horseradish, chopped egg and cream mixture. The cooked beef (in strips), beans and tomatoes are set in aspic, and unmolded into the shells

Menu 3

TIMETABLE

Day before
Roast beef fillet for flan, let cool and cover; make aspic — keep both in refrigerator.
Make pastry dough for flan and keep in plastic bag in refrigerator.
Make raspberry sauce for strawberries and keep in refrigerator.

Morning
Set beef with aspic in pans, cover and chill.
Roll out pastry dough for flan and bake shells; keep covered.
Make horseradish mixture for beef flan and chill.
Make potato and zucchini salads and chill.
Hull strawberries, add sauce, cover and chill.

Just before serving
Spread horseradish mixture in flans and unmold aspic into them.
Transfer the salads to serving dishes.

Entrée

Steak Flan

For rich pie pastry
4 cups flour
1 teaspoon salt
$\frac{3}{4}$ cup butter
$\frac{1}{2}$ cup shortening
2 egg yolks
6–8 tablespoons water

For filling
3 lb fillet of beef
2–3 tablespoons oil
1 lb green beans, trimmed
$\frac{1}{4}$ cup grated fresh horseradish
   or $\frac{1}{2}$ cup prepared
   horseradish
4 eggs, hard-cooked and
   chopped
1$\frac{1}{2}$ cups heavy cream, whipped
   until it holds a soft shape
salt and pepper
$\frac{1}{4}$ teaspoon dry mustard
   (or to taste)
8 cups cool but still liquid aspic
6–7 medium tomatoes, peeled,
   quartered, and seeds
   removed

*Two 10 inch flan rings; two
   9 inch springform pans or
   deep cake pans*

Method
Set oven at hot (400°F). Make pie pastry dough and chill for 30 minutes.
   Roll out dough and line the flan rings. Bake in heated oven for 10–12 minutes; turn down oven to moderately hot (375°F) and continue baking 15 minutes or until browned.
   To roast the fillet of beef: set the oven at hot (400°F). Heat the oil in a roasting pan, add the fillet and baste with oil; turn and baste again. Lift meat onto a rack in the pan and roast for 45 minutes in a hot oven or until a meat thermometer inserted in the center

registers 140°F (for rare beef). Cool, then cut in strips.
   Cook the beans in boiling salted water for 15 minutes or until tender; drain, refresh and drain again. Stir the horseradish and chopped eggs into the lightly whipped cream and season well with salt, pepper and mustard.
   Set the springform or deep cake pan in a roasting pan filled with water and ice, add a $\frac{3}{4}$ inch layer of cool but still liquid aspic and chill until firmly set. Arrange the beef, beans and tomatoes in the pan and add enough aspic almost to cover them. Let stand until set, add remaining aspic and chill in the refrigerator at least 2 hours or until firmly set.
   To serve: set pastry shells on platters and spread the horseradish mixture in the bottom of each shell. Unmold the beef in aspic into the pastry shells; cut in wedges to serve. Serve potato salad and zucchini salad separately.

Accompaniment to entrée

Zucchini Salad

2 lb small zucchini
$\frac{1}{2}$ cup olive oil
4 shallots, finely chopped
1 tablespoon paprika
salt and pepper
1 teaspoon sugar
2 teaspoons dill seed or
   chopped fresh dill
$\frac{1}{4}$ cup wine vinegar

Method
Wipe the zucchini and slice them thinly. In a skillet, heat the oil, add the shallot and zucchini and cook over low heat for 5 minutes. Add the paprika, seasoning, sugar, dill

and vinegar and continue cooking 5 more minutes or until the zucchini is just tender. Season to taste and chill.

Dessert

Strawberries Cardinal

3 quarts fresh strawberries,
   hulled
4 quarts fresh raspberries or
   4 packages frozen
   raspberries
$\frac{1}{2}$–1 cup confectioners' sugar
   (or to taste)
$\frac{1}{3}$ cup kirsch
1 cup Chantilly cream (made
   with $\frac{1}{2}$ cup heavy cream,
   1 tablespoon sugar and
   $\frac{1}{2}$ teaspoon vanilla)—optional

Method
Sieve the raspberries or purée them in a blender and strain to remove the seeds. Beat in confectioners' sugar to taste with the kirsch (frozen raspberries need very little sugar).
   Pile the strawberries in a bowl and spoon the sauce over them. Cover and chill at least 2 hours before serving.
   Serve the strawberries in a large glass bowl or in individual serving bowls, topped with Chantilly cream, if you like.

Ingredients for cocido Madrileño, a meat, fowl and vegetable stew from Madrid (recipe is on page 122)

SPANISH AND PORTUGUESE COOKING

The massive barrier of the Pyrenees effectively separates Spain and Portugal from the rest of Europe. The cooking reflects this isolation. Not only is French cuisine forgotten 20 miles over the border, but also communications within the Iberian peninsula are poor, and regions like the Basque country and Catalonia have their own language as well as their own cuisine.

Despite this diversity, however, there are many common themes. Cocido, for example, is regarded as Spain's national dish. The classic recipe from Madrid (cocido Madrileño) is a huge stew of pork, beef, spicy chorizo sausage, chicken, chick-peas, potatoes, carrots, cabbage and onions, all flavored with a ham bone. The cooking broth is strained and simmered with noodles to serve as soup, then the vegetables are served as a separate course, followed by the chicken and meats.

Garlic is the all-pervasive seasoning in Spain and Portugal and the quantities can sometimes disconcert an unaccustomed palate. Garlic soup, flavored with paprika and thickened with bread, is a favorite in Spain (the Portuguese version adds fresh coriander) and ali-oli, a pungent garlic mayonnaise, is served everywhere. In both countries, olive oil is a primary ingredient; butter is a luxury. In Portugal, the traditional trade with Africa and the Orient has encouraged the use of spices like curry and hot peppers called piri-piri.

By American standards, everything is late in Spain and Portugal. Lunch is served at 2 or 3 p.m., so those who rise early often have a mid-morning snack of sausage with bread or a cup of chocolate with a stick of churros (fried crullers) or buñuelos (doughnuts).

In towns a late morning aperitif is the rule, accompanied by tapas (hors d'oeuvre). These may simply consist of a few salted almonds or olives but often extend to a dozen or more tempting little dishes. Lunch is substantial, with at least three courses and this necessitates a siesta, so work does not begin again until 4. Supper or dinner is also late — in Madrid it is often in full swing at midnight — so early evening snacks are common.

Eating in these two countries cannot be considered without drinking. The ports of Oporto, the sherries of Jerez and the wine of the Portuguese island of Madeira are the most famous fortified wines in the world and they are enjoyed at all times of the day.

111

Regional Specialties

Cocido is the most popular of the many Iberian dishes that are cooked in one pot. From Galicia in the northwest comes caldo Gallego, a soup made with dried beans, ham, pork, potatoes and turnips. The famous paella from Valencia combines chicken, fish and vegetables with glowing, saffron-flavored baked rice.

Fish stews are made all along the coast. Both Catalonia and the Basque country boast the colorfully named zarzuela (light operetta) made from crayfish, shrimps, mussels, squid and several kinds of white fish, all simmered with tomatoes and flavored with ground almonds and saffron. The Basque version substitutes cayenne and cognac for the Catalonian saffron.

Portugal has a worthy rival to zarzuela with its caldeirada — a fisherman's stew that basically consists of white fish and shellfish, simmered with white wine and tomatoes, and often flavored with chopped fresh coriander.

In fact, fish is of great importance throughout the Iberian peninsula where, until recently, pork was the only meat most of the population could afford. Even in areas far from the coast, salt cod is still a staple and cooks make more imaginative use of it than anywhere else in the world.

The central plateau around Madrid is known as the region of roasting because of the excellence of its suckling pigs, baby lamb, beef and game. In the east, near Valencia, the balmy Mediterranean climate permits the growing of rice and, further south, Seville is renowned for its bitter oranges used for preserves. The north-ern coast, swept by winds from the Bay of Biscay, is less hospitable, and the food of Galicia in the northwest is less refined than elsewhere.

Manuel Pena, our Spanish and Portuguese **cooking consultant**, has a native flair for Iberian cuisine. He has followed the cooking traditions of his Galician-born parents and now manages the 50-year-old family grocery store, Casa Pena, in Washington, D.C.

Mr. Pena is regarded by the Washington diplomatic community as a leading expert on the proper customs and eating habits of Spain and Portugal and frequently advises the local embassies on entertainment. His favorite dish is caldo Gallego from his native province (recipe is on page 115).

Tapas
(Hors d'œuvre)

Tapas are a Spanish institution. Even the most modest bar offers a few nuts or olives with drinks and many have a tempting array of such snacks as pickled vegetables, sausages, fish and shellfish, snails, empanadillas (little turnovers), hard-cooked eggs in various sauces, miniature kebabs called banderillas, and thinly sliced serrano ham (similar to prosciutto).

Some bars go to great lengths to provide dozens of tapas, including quite substantial dishes like squid in its ink, stewed variety meats or pigs' feet. The following recipes are typical — each serves 4 people.

Empanadillas
(Miniature Turnovers)

2 cups flour
1 teaspoon salt
$\frac{1}{4}$ cup olive oil
1 egg
5 tablespoons water
1 egg, beaten to mix with
    $\frac{1}{2}$ teaspoon salt (for glaze)
choice of filling (see right)

$2\frac{1}{2}$–3 inch cookie cutter

Makes 34–36 empanadillas.

Method
Sift the flour with the salt onto a board or marble slab, make a well in the center and add the oil, egg and water. Work the central ingredients with the fingertips until mixed, then draw in the flour with the whole hand, adding more water if necessary to form a smooth dough. Knead the dough lightly, wrap and chill 30 minutes.

Set oven at hot (400°F).

Roll the dough thinly and cut out $2\frac{1}{2}$–3 inch rounds with a cookie cutter. Add 1 teaspoon of your chosen filling, brush the edges with water, fold in half and press the edges firmly together to seal them. Brush the turnovers with egg glaze and bake in the heated oven for 15 minutes or until they are brown. Serve them hot or cold.

Turnovers can also be fried in hot deep fat until browned. Then they should not be brushed with glaze and are best eaten at once.

Suggested Fillings for Empanadillas

Slice of chorizo sausage.
Cubes of cooked ham.
Ground cooked ham moistened with tomato sauce.
Cooked fish, flaked and bound with white sauce.
Chopped cooked clams mixed with tomato sauce.
Chopped hard-cooked egg mixed with finely chopped anchovy.

Banderillas
(Miniature Kebabs)

On small kebab skewers thread any combination of olives, pickled carrots, pickled sweet peppers, and cooked clams, scallops, shrimps, sardines, eel, anchovy, ham, sausage and cheese.

An attractive selection of tapas (Spanish hors d'oeuvre) includes banderillas (miniature kebabs), Catalan shrimps and browned mussels (top row); chorizo sausage with lentil purée, empanadillas (miniature turnovers) and roasted peanuts (center row); cauliflower in garlic mayonnaise, ripe olives and serraño ham around vegetables (bottom row)

Mejillones Gratinados
(Browned Mussels)

3 quarts large mussels
½ cup white wine

For topping
1 cup fresh white breadcrumbs
2 cloves of garlic, crushed
¼ cup olive oil
3 tablespoons chopped parsley
salt
black pepper, freshly ground

Method
Scrub mussel shells thoroughly, discarding any that do not close when tapped.

Put mussels in a kettle, pour over the wine, cover and cook over high heat for 5–7 minutes or until the shells open, stirring once. Take pan from heat, cool slightly, then discard the top shell of the mussels and gristly 'beard' or ring around the edge of the shell; discard any mussels that do not open. Strain the cooking liquid through cheesecloth and reserve it.

To make the topping: fry the breadcrumbs with the garlic in the oil until browned; season well and stir in the parsley.

Spoon the mixture on top of the mussels and set them in a heatproof baking dish. Spoon over the reserved cooking liquid and bake the mussels in a hot oven (400°F) for 10–12 minutes or until very hot. Serve them hot or cold.

Coliflor con Ali-oli
(Cauliflower in Garlic Mayonnaise)

1 cauliflower, divided into sprigs
few pitted black olives (for garnish)
1 tablespoon chopped parsley (for sprinkling)

For garlic mayonnaise
4–5 cloves of garlic
1 tablespoon lemon juice or 2 tablespoons vinegar
2 egg yolks
1 cup olive oil
salt and pepper

Method
Cook the cauliflower in boiling salted water for 8–10 minutes or until just tender. Drain and leave to cool.

To make the garlic mayonnaise: pound garlic with half the lemon juice or vinegar and a pinch of salt in a mortar and pestle or crush in a bowl with the end of a rolling pin. Beat in the egg yolks and continue beating until slightly thickened. Add the olive oil, a drop or two at a time until the mayonnaise is quite thick. Once the mayonnaise starts to thicken, the oil can be added a little faster. When mayonnaise is very thick, add remaining lemon juice, and continue beating in the oil until all is added. Taste the mayonnaise for seasoning and add a little warm water if it is very thick.

Pile the cauliflower in a bowl and spoon over the mayonnaise. Garnish with olives and sprinkle with parsley. Serve cold.

Langostinos a la Catalana
(Catalan Shrimps)

1 lb cooked peeled shrimps

For sauce
1 onion, finely chopped
3 tablespoons olive oil
3 tomatoes, peeled, seeded and chopped
½ cup white wine
pinch of saffron soaked in 2 tablespoons boiling water
pinch of cayenne
salt and pepper
1 red bell pepper, skinned, cored and cut in strips

Method
To make the sauce: in a skillet fry the onion in the oil until soft. Add the tomatoes, wine, saffron and water, cayenne and seasoning and simmer, stirring, for 12–15 minutes or until the mixture is thick. Add the red pepper 5 minutes before the end of cooking. Let the sauce cool and serve with the shrimps piled on top.

Chorizo con Salsa de Lentejas
(Chorizo Sausage with Lentil Purée)

1 lb chorizo sausage, cut in 2–3 inch lengths
½ cup (¼ lb) lentils, soaked overnight and drained
2 green peppers, cored, seeded and cut into strips
¼ lb piece of bacon or fresh pork fat, diced
1 bay leaf
salt and pepper

Method
In a flameproof casserole fry the bacon or pork until browned and the fat is rendered. Discard bacon or pork fat. Add the lentils and bay leaf, cover with warm water, add the lid and simmer 1½ hours or until the lentils are almost tender.

Add the green pepper and cook 10 minutes longer. Discard the bay leaf and work the mixture through a sieve or purée it in a blender. The mixture should be fairly liquid.

Add the sausages, salt and pepper, if needed, cover and cook 15–20 minutes longer. Lift out the sausages.

Serve the lentil purée hot or cold with the sausages.

To Peel Bell Peppers

Broil the pepper or hold it with a two-pronged fork over a flame until the thin skin is charred all over. Using a knife, peel off the skin and rinse the pepper under running water, if necessary.

114

Caldo Gallego
(Galician White Bean Soup)

1 cup ($\frac{1}{2}$ lb) dried white kidney
   beans, soaked overnight
   and drained
2 quarts water
$\frac{1}{4}$ lb serraño ham or prosciutto,
   diced (see box)
$\frac{1}{4}$ lb piece of salt pork or bacon
2–3 white turnips, cut in large
   pieces
$\frac{1}{2}$ lb turnip greens, cut in
   large pieces
1 potato, cut in large pieces
$\frac{1}{4}$ lb chorizo sausage
   (optional)
salt
black pepper, freshly ground

Method
Blanch the salt pork or bacon by putting it in cold water, bringing to a boil and draining. Cut it in cubes.

   In a kettle put the drained beans with the water, ham and salt pork or bacon, cover and simmer 2 hours. Add the turnips, turnip greens, potato, sausage, if used, and seasoning, cover and simmer $\frac{1}{2}$ hour longer or until the vegetables and beans are tender.

   Cut the sausage in slices, replace them in the soup and taste for seasoning.

Serraño ham is a raw smoked ham similar to Italian prosciutto, but with a sweeter flavor. It is not imported into the United States. Prosciutto, or any other smoked ham can be substituted. When large chunks of ham are called for, use Smithfield ham.

Sopa de Ajo
(Spanish Garlic Soup)

4 cloves of garlic
$\frac{1}{3}$ cup olive oil
6 thin slices of white bread
1 teaspoon paprika
5 cups boiling water
salt
black pepper, freshly ground
4 eggs
2 teaspoons chopped parsley
   (for garnish)

In Spain, after frying the garlic cloves in oil, many cooks crush them and add them to the soup with the water. This gives the soup quite a strong garlic flavor, so you may prefer to discard them as suggested below.

Method
In a kettle fry the garlic cloves in the oil over low heat until browned and the oil has absorbed the flavor of the garlic. Discard the garlic. Add the bread and fry until browned.

   Take the pan from the heat and stir in the paprika. Add the water and seasoning, cover and simmer the soup for 12–15 minutes until the bread is broken up and thickens the soup. During cooking, crush the bread against the sides of the pan to help it break up.

   Taste the soup for seasoning and spoon it into heatproof bowls. Drop an egg in each bowl and bake the soup in a hot oven (400°F) for 5 minutes or until the egg whites are set but the yolks are still soft. Sprinkle each bowl with parsley and serve.

Gazpacho

Gazpacho is essentially a liquid salad. The most famous version from Andalusia uses tomatoes, cucumber and green pepper and is thickened with breadcrumbs. In the south, around Jerez, chopped raw onions are added, while near Cordoba the soup is white and made of olive oil, vinegar, water, garlic and almonds. Often, but not always, ice is added before the soup is served.

   The following recipe for gazpacho comes from Alicante and two others are given in Volumes 15 and 18.

Gazpacho Alicantina

4 cups chicken stock
1 clove of garlic, crushed
$\frac{1}{2}$ large red onion, thinly sliced
1 large tomato, peeled and
   seeded
1 cucumber, peeled and
   seeded
$\frac{1}{2}$ red bell pepper, cored and
   seeded
$\frac{1}{2}$ green pepper, cored and
   seeded
juice of $\frac{1}{2}$ lemon
2 tablespoons olive oil
   salt
black pepper, freshly ground

Method
Combine the stock, garlic and onion in a pan. Cover and simmer 5 minutes. Strain the mixture through a fine sieve and chill.

   Cut the tomato, cucumber and peppers into very small dice and stir into the chicken stock mixture with the lemon juice, olive oil and seasoning to taste. Chill thoroughly before serving.

Caldo Verde
(Portuguese Kale Soup)

1 lb fresh kale, shredded
3 potatoes, peeled and thinly
   sliced
1 medium onion, thinly sliced
1 quart water
salt
¼ lb linguiça or chouriço
   sausages (see box)
⅓ cup olive oil
black pepper, freshly ground

Caldo verde is always served with a hearty yeast bread, made with finely ground cornmeal.

Method
Put the potatoes and onion with the water and a little salt in a kettle, cover and bring to a boil. Simmer 10–15 minutes or until the potatoes are very tender.

Fry the sausages in 1 tablespoon olive oil until browned, add ¼ cup water, cover and cook gently for 10–15 minutes. Let cool and cut them in thin slices.

Lift out vegetables from water with a slotted spoon and mash them with a potato masher or fork. Return them to the cooking water with the remaining olive oil, greens and pepper, bring to a boil and simmer 3–4 minutes or until the kale is just tender; taste for seasoning.

Put 2–3 slices of sausage in each soup bowl, pour over the soup and serve.

Chorizo is a spicy Spanish sausage flavored with pimiento, red pepper and garlic; the Portuguese version is called **chouriço**. Chorizo is available in many specialty stores.

Linguiça is another Portuguese sausage flavored with cinnamon, cumin, garlic and red pepper, cured in vinegar pickle and heavily smoked. It is longer than chorizo and has a coarser texture.

Tortilla
(Omelet)

Spanish tortilla is a flat omelet that is browned on both sides. It has nothing to do with Mexican tortilla bread except that both are round and flat.

The filling for the omelet — ham, onion, potato and tomato are favorites — is usually fried, then added to the eggs and heated again in the omelet. Sometimes two omelets are sandwiched with a sauce as in tortilla Barcelonesa.

Basic Tortilla

7–8 eggs
salt
black pepper, freshly ground
3 tablespoons olive oil
chosen filling (see right)

Serves 3–4.

Method
Make the filling and let it cool to tepid.

Beat the eggs with salt and pepper to taste in a bowl and stir in the filling.

In an 8–9 inch omelet pan heat the oil, quickly stir egg mixture and pour it into the pan. Cook over medium heat, shaking the pan and loosening the edges of the omelet with a spatula so it does not stick.

When it is almost set in the center and well browned underneath, put a plate over the pan and turn the omelet out onto it. Slide the omelet back into the pan and cook 1 minute longer or until the underside is browned. Transfer to a platter and cut in wedges to serve.

Tortilla de Patata
(Potato Omelet)

Thinly slice 3 peeled potatoes and fry them in ¼ cup olive oil, stirring occasionally, until they begin to brown. Add 1 onion, finely chopped, sprinkle with seasoning and continue cooking until the potatoes and onion are browned.

Make an omelet as described in basic tortilla, using 4 eggs and 2 tablespoons olive oil.

Tortilla Balear
(Sardine Omelet)

Drain 1 can sardines of oil, split them in half, lengthwise, and discard the backbone. Fry ½ onion, finely chopped, with 1 clove of garlic, crushed, in 1 tablespoon olive oil until soft. Sprinkle the mixture over the sardines with the juice of ½ lemon.

Make an omelet with 7–8 eggs and add half the eggs to the pan. When lightly set on the bottom, lay the sardine mixture on top, pour over the remaining eggs and finish as for basic tortilla.

Tortilla Granadina
(Chicken Liver Omelet)

Cut 1 cup chicken livers in ¼ inch slices and fry in 3 tablespoons olive oil until they are lightly browned. Add 1 clove of garlic, crushed, 2 tablespoons chopped parsley and ½ cup white wine and simmer 5 minutes until mixture is fairly thick.

Make the omelet as described in basic tortilla, using 7–8 eggs.

Tortilla a la Jardinera
(Gardener's Omelet)

In a skillet fry 1 onion, chopped, in 3 tablespoons olive oil until soft. Add 1 clove of garlic, crushed, and 1½–2 cups of mixed vegetables — such as chopped cooked carrot, cooked green peas, chopped cooked green beans and peeled, seeded and chopped tomatoes. Season and heat well, stirring.

Make an omelet as described in basic tortilla, using 7–8 eggs.

Tortilla a la jardinera is filled with cooked mixed vegetables

Caldeirada is Portuguese fisherman's stew, and includes a colorful variety of white fish, clams, eel, squid and large shrimps

Pisto

Pisto is a vegetable stew usually based on peppers, tomatoes, onions and squash, though beans and peas may also be added.

In some versions lightly beaten eggs are stirred into the vegetables at the end of cooking and heated until they are lightly scrambled.

Pisto Manchego
(La Mancha Vegetable Stew)

¼ cup olive oil
3 onions, thinly sliced
2 cloves of garlic, crushed
1 red pepper, cored, seeded and thinly sliced
1 green pepper, cored, seeded and thinly sliced
salt
black pepper, freshly ground
2 tomatoes, peeled, seeded and chopped
2 zucchini, cut in ¼ inch slices or 1 small eggplant, diced
6 eggs (optional), beaten to mix

If eggs are added, pisto makes a good supper dish. Without eggs it is usually served as an accompaniment to roast meat.

Method
If using eggplant, sprinkle it with salt and let stand 15 minutes to draw out the bitter juices (dégorger). Rinse with cold water and drain well.

In a skillet heat the oil and fry the onions with the garlic until soft but not browned. Add the red and green peppers with seasoning. Cook over low heat for 5 minutes. Add the tomatoes and zucchini or eggplant and continue cooking slowly, stirring occasionally, for 10–15 min-

utes or until the vegetables are tender. Taste for seasoning.

If adding eggs, pour them into the pan with the cooked vegetables, and cook, stirring, until lightly scrambled. Serve at once.

Caldeirada
(Portuguese Fishermen's Stew)

3 quarts hard shell clams
3 lb white fish steaks and fillets (haddock, cod, sole, red snapper, bass)
3–4 squid, cleaned and cut up (see box)
1 lb fresh eel, cut in 2-inch slices
8 large shrimps
½ cup olive oil
3 medium onions, finely chopped
5 tomatoes, peeled, seeded and chopped
3 cloves of garlic, crushed
6 medium potatoes, sliced
salt
black pepper, freshly ground
2 cups white wine
2 cups water
⅓ cup chopped fresh coriander (cilantro) or parsley

A wide variety of white fish should be used for this stew. This recipe serves 8 people.

Method
Scrub the clams thoroughly and discard any that do not close when tapped. Cut the white fish into 2-inch pieces, discarding some skin and bone (in Portugal skin and bones are often left in the stew to add flavor). Mix the onion, tomatoes and garlic.

Pour the oil in a large kettle or flameproof casserole. Add the clams and sprinkle with half the onion mixture; season well. Add a layer of pieces of

white fish, squid, eel and potatoes, put in the shrimps and top with remaining onion and tomato mixture, fish and potatoes, sprinkling each layer with seasoning.

Pour over the wine and water, cover and bring to a boil. Simmer 20 minutes or until the clams are open and the fish flakes when tested with a fork; discard any clams that do not open.

Stir the stew once to mix the ingredients, sprinkle with chopped coriander or parsley and serve in bowls. Shrimp and clam shells are generally removed at the table.

Langosta a la Barcelonesa
(Spiny Lobster from Barcelona)

4 live spiny lobsters (1–1¼ lb each)
½ cup olive oil
juice of ½ lemon

For sauce
¼ cup olive oil
4 tomatoes, peeled, seeded and finely chopped
3 cloves of garlic, crushed
2 tablespoons chopped parsley
¼ cup brandy
1 cup white wine
¼ teaspoon nutmeg
1 cup water
salt and pepper

Regular clawed lobsters or rock lobster tails can be substituted for live spiny lobsters in this dish.

Method
To make the sauce: in a saucepan heat the oil, add the tomatoes, garlic and parsley and cook over medium heat until the tomatoes are pulpy. Add the brandy, wine, nut-

meg, water and seasoning and simmer 15 minutes or until the sauce is fairly thick. Taste for seasoning and keep warm.

To kill lobsters with a knife: lay the lobster flat on a board, hard shell up, with the head facing to the right, tail to the left; cover the tail with a cloth. Hold lobster firmly behind the head with your left hand and, with the point of a sharp chopping knife, pierce down to the board through the cross mark that lies on the center of the head.

Continue cutting through the body and tail until the lobster is split in half. Discard the head sac and intestinal tract but reserve the green tomalley and any black coral (this will turn bright red on cooking). Repeat with remaining lobsters. If using clawed lobsters, crack the claws.

Set the lobsters on a broiler rack, cut side up, and sprinkle with olive oil, lemon juice, salt and pepper. Broil about 4 inches from the flame for 10–12 minutes or until the lobster meat is tender; brush with more olive oil during broiling. Spoon the sauce over the lobsters and serve at once.

To Clean Squid
Slit open belly and remove bone. Immerse squid in warm water and pull off purplish outer skin. Remove sac of dark ink from near the bone, rinse squid thoroughly. Cut tentacles in 1-inch pieces and body into rings.

Paella

There are many versions of paella, all based on saffron rice; often meat, fowl and fish are added as well as vegetables.

Cooking is done in a shallow two-handled pan — a paella pan — and the mixture is brought quickly to a boil, then simmered until the rice has absorbed all the liquid and the flavors of the different ingredients are blended together. Two other versions of paella were given in Volume 2.

Paella Valenciana

1 cup rice
1 quart large mussels
$\frac{1}{4}$ cup olive oil
4 chicken pieces
$\frac{1}{4}$ lb lean pork or ham, cut in cubes
1 onion, chopped
1 green pepper, cored, seeded and cut in strips
1 clove of garlic, crushed
2 tomatoes, peeled, seeded and chopped
salt and pepper
2 cups water
large pinch of saffron (soaked in 2–3 tablespoons hot water for 20 minutes)
$\frac{1}{2}$ cup sliced chorizo sausage
$\frac{1}{2}$ cup fresh or frozen green peas
$\frac{1}{2}$ cup green beans, cut in 1-inch lengths
4 large shrimps

12–14 inch diameter paella pan or shallow flameproof casserole

Method
Scrub the shells of the mussels in cold water and discard any that do not close when tapped.

Heat the oil in the paella pan or casserole and fry the pieces of chicken over medium heat until browned on all sides, allowing 10–12 minutes. Take them out, add the pork or ham and brown lightly.

Add the onion, green pepper, garlic, tomatoes and seasoning and cook, stirring occasionally, until the vegetables are tender and all liquid has evaporated; lift out with a slotted spoon.

Add the rice to the pan and cook, stirring, until hot and coated with any remaining oil. Add water and saffron with its liquid and bring to a boil.

Take from the heat and put the chicken pieces, green pepper mixture, sausage slices, peas, beans, mussels and shrimps on top of the rice. Bring quickly back to a boil and simmer on top of the stove or bake in a moderate oven (350°F) for 20–25 minutes or until all liquid is absorbed and the mussels have opened.

Let paella stand in a warm place for 5 minutes for the flavors to blend, taste for seasoning and serve.

Zarzuela
(Basque Fish Stew)

$1\frac{1}{4}$–$1\frac{1}{2}$ lb live lobster
1 lb white fish (whiting, hake, red snapper, bass)
2–3 small squid
2 quarts hard shell clams
2 tablespoons olive oil
1 onion, finely chopped
2 cloves of garlic, crushed
3 tomatoes, peeled, seeded and chopped
$\frac{1}{4}$ teaspoon cayenne
salt
black pepper, freshly ground
1 cup white wine
1 cup water
6 large shrimps
$\frac{1}{4}$ cup brandy

Serves 6.

Method
To kill lobster with a knife: lay the lobster flat on a board, hard shell up, with the head facing to the right, tail to the left; cover the tail with a cloth. Hold lobster firmly behind the head with your left hand and, with the point of a sharp knife, pierce down to the board through the cross mark that lies on the center of the head. Continue cutting through the body to the tail and cut off the tail in one piece.

Cut the lobster tail crosswise, into 1-inch slices (scallops), including the shell, and detach and crack the claws. Discard the head sac and intestinal tract from the body of the lobster.

Cut white fish into 2-inch pieces, discarding skin and bone. Clean and cut up squid (see page 119). Scrub the clams thoroughly and discard any that do not close when tapped. Place clams in a saucepan, cover and cook over high heat, stirring once, for 5 minutes or until the shells open. Remove the top shells and discard any clams that do not open.

In a kettle heat the oil and fry the onion and garlic until soft but not browned. Add the tomatoes, cayenne and seasoning; cook to a thick pulp.

Add the wine and water and bring to a boil. Add the lobster, squid, white fish and shrimps, cover and simmer 10 minutes. Put the clams on top, and continue cooking, uncovered, until the fish and lobster are cooked.

Spoon over the brandy and let stand 5 minutes in a warm place. Taste for seasoning and serve. Shrimp, lobster and clam shells are generally removed at the table.

Bacalao a la Vizcaina
(Basque Salt Cod)

$1\frac{1}{2}$ lb salt cod
4–5 small dried red peppers
1 slice of white bread
$\frac{1}{2}$ cup olive oil
1 large onion, chopped
3–4 cloves of garlic, crushed
4–5 tomatoes, peeled, seeded and chopped
3 canned pimientos, drained and chopped
black pepper, freshly ground
salt (optional)
$\frac{1}{2}$ cup fresh white breadcrumbs
$\frac{1}{4}$ cup flour seasoned with $\frac{1}{4}$ teaspoon salt and pinch of pepper
1 tablespoon chopped parsley

Method
Soak the cod for about 8 hours in several changes of cold water. Drain, remove the bones and skin and divide the fish into serving-sized pieces. Blanch cod by putting in cold water, bringing to a boil and draining thoroughly.

Discard the stems and seeds from the peppers, cut them into small pieces and soak in 2–3 cups boiling water for 30 minutes. Drain.

Brown the slice of bread on both sides in 1–2 tablespoons of the oil, drain and crush to crumbs.

In a saucepan heat 2 tablespoons more oil and fry the onion very slowly until soft. Add the garlic, tomatoes, pimientos and black pepper, cover and simmer, stirring occasionally until the tomatoes are pulpy. Work the mixture through a strainer and stir in the fresh breadcrumbs. Coat the cod with the seasoned flour.

Heat the remaining oil in a skillet and brown the cod on both sides. Pour a layer of sauce in a casserole, place the fish on top and spoon over the remaining sauce. Sprinkle with fried breadcrumbs and bake in a moderate oven (350°F) for 35–45 minutes or until the cod flakes easily. Shake the pan from time to time to prevent the fish from sticking. Sprinkle the cod with chopped parsley just before serving.

The Basque country is particularly famous for its food. In this northern corner of the Pyrenees ingredients are limited but clever use of seasonings and hotter spices than are the rule elsewhere have made dishes like bacalao vizcaina well known all over Spain.

Bacalhau Portuguêsa
(Portuguese Salt Cod)

1½ lb salt cod
1 cup dried garbanzos (chickpeas), soaked overnight and drained
salt
½ cup olive oil
2 onions, chopped
2 cloves of garlic, crushed
½ cup white wine vinegar
1 teaspoon paprika
few drops of Tabasco
black pepper, freshly ground

For garnish
1 green pepper, cored, seeded and very finely chopped
¼ cup ripe olives
¼ cup green olives
1 tablespoon olive oil
1 tablespoon chopped fresh coriander

Method
Put the drained garbanzos in a pan with plenty of water, cover and simmer 1½ hours. Add salt and cook ½–1 hour longer or until the garbanzos are tender. Drain them.

Soak the cod for about 8 hours in several changes of cold water. Drain and put in a pan with water to cover, add a lid and simmer 15–20 minutes or until the fish flakes easily. Drain and flake, discarding bones and skin.

In a large skillet heat the oil, add onion, cod, garbanzos, garlic, vinegar, paprika, Tabasco and black pepper. Heat gently, stirring, until the mixture is very hot. Taste for seasoning, add salt, if needed, and keep warm.

To prepare the garnish: fry the pepper in the oil over high heat until just soft and arrange around the edge of a platter.

Pile the cod mixture in the center and decorate with both kinds of olives. Sprinkle with chopped coriander and serve.

Portuguese salt cod is garnished with green peppers, olives and chopped fresh coriander

Pollo Chilindrón
(Spanish Chicken with Ham and Peppers)

3½-4 lb roasting chicken, cut
  in pieces
¼ cup olive oil
1 onion, chopped
2 cloves of garlic, crushed
4 red bell peppers, peeled,
  cored, seeded and cut in
  strips (see page 114)
¼ lb serraño ham, chopped
3 tomatoes, peeled, seeded
  and chopped
black pepper, freshly ground
salt

Method
In a skillet or shallow flame-proof casserole heat the oil and brown the chicken pieces on all sides over medium heat. Remove them, add the onion and garlic and cook until soft.

Add the peppers, ham, tomatoes and seasoning and cook, stirring occasionally, until the tomatoes are pulpy.
Watchpoint: if the ham is salty, very little extra salt will be needed.

Replace the pieces of chicken and spoon some sauce on top of them. Cover and cook over low heat for 20–25 minutes or until the chicken is very tender.

Frango Portuguêsa
(Portuguese Chicken with Rice)

4–5 lb roasting chicken or fowl
1¼ cups rice
2 onions
6 whole cloves
3-inch stick of cinnamon
½ teaspoon whole coriander
  seeds
10 peppercorns
pinch of saffron soaked for 20
  minutes in 2 tablespoons
  boiling water
2 cloves of garlic, peeled
salt and pepper
2 tablespoons olive oil
1 tablespoon chopped fresh
  coriander or parsley
  (for sprinkling)

Trussing needle and string

Method
Truss the bird and put it in a kettle with 1 onion, stuck with the cloves, the cinnamon, whole coriander seeds, peppercorns, saffron and liquid and garlic.

Add water to cover, season with a little salt and simmer until the bird is almost tender, allowing about 1 hour for the roasting chicken or 1½ hours for fowl. Strain off and reserve 2½ cups cooking broth.

In a flameproof casserole fry the remaining onion, chopped, in the oil until soft but not brown. Add the rice and cook, stirring, until the grains are coated with oil and look transparent. Add the reserved broth and seasoning, cover and simmer 20 minutes. Let stand in a warm place 10 minutes before stirring with a fork and tasting for seasoning.

When the chicken is tender, drain it, set it on a platter and pile rice around. Sprinkle with coriander or parsley and serve.

Cocido Madrileño
(Madrid Meat, Fowl and Vegetable Stew)

½ lb piece bacon or salt pork
2 lb eye of round or sirloin tip
  of beef, tied
4–5 lb fowl or roasting chicken
1 cup dried garbanzos (chick-
  peas), soaked overnight and
  drained
1 ham bone
3 cloves of garlic, crushed
3 quarts water
black pepper, freshly ground
8 small carrots
2 onions, quartered
4 medium leeks, halved
  lengthwise
1 lb chorizo sausage
3 medium potatoes, quartered
2–3 medium turnips, quartered
1 medium cabbage, cut in
  8 wedges
salt (optional)
½ cup fine vermicelli noodles

A good cocido is not easy to achieve — the broth must be rich and well balanced so no single taste predominates; each vegetable must be cooked to just the right stage and the meats should be very tender without overcooking so the flavor is not lost.

Method
Blanch the bacon or salt pork by putting it in cold water, bringing to a boil and draining.

In a kettle put the bacon or salt pork, beef, fowl, if using, drained garbanzos, ham bone, garlic, water and black pepper. Bring to a boil, skim, cover and simmer 1 hour. If using a roasting chicken, add it and continue simmering ½ hour; add the carrots and simmer 15 minutes longer. Add the onions and leeks and simmer 10 minutes longer.

Simmer the chorizo sau-sage in water for 10 minutes and drain. Add the sausage to the kettle along with the potatoes, turnips and cabbage and simmer 15 minutes longer or until all the vegetables and meats are very tender.

Strain off the broth, and taste for seasoning — if the ham bone was salty, more salt may not be needed. Add the vermicelli noodles to the broth and simmer 6–7 minutes or until they are just tender.

Meanwhile arrange the vegetables on a platter and keep warm. Carve the fowl or chicken and slice the beef, sausage and bacon or salt pork. Arrange the chicken, meats and sausage, on a platter, cover and keep warm. Serve the broth, followed by the vegetables, with the meats as a third course.

Portuguese chicken with rice is sprinkled with fresh coriander or parsley for serving

Porco Alentejana
(Portuguese Pork with Clams)

1½ lb boneless lean pork, cut
   in 1-inch cubes
2 quarts hard shell clams
1 tablespoon paprika
2 tablespoons lard
2 tablespoons olive oil
1 onion, chopped
2 tomatoes, peeled, seeded
   and chopped
1 bay leaf
few drops of Tabasco
salt
black pepper, freshly ground

For garnish
1 tablespoon chopped
   coriander or chopped parsley
1 lemon, cut in wedges

Method
Toss the pork in the paprika
until coated and let stand ½–1
hour. Scrub the clams thoroughly in cold water and discard any that do not close
when tapped.

   In a skillet heat the lard
and fry the pork over fairly
low heat, stirring occasionally
for 15–20 minutes or until
tender. In a large pan heat the
oil, add the onion and fry until
soft. Add the tomatoes, bay
leaf, Tabasco and seasoning
and cook, stirring occasionally, until the mixture is pulpy.

   Add the clams, cover and
cook over high heat, stirring
once or twice, until the clams
open. Add the pork, stir to
mix, cover and cook gently
for 5 minutes.

   Discard the bay leaf, sprinkle with coriander or parsley
and serve with lemon wedges.
Boiled potatoes or croûtes of
fried bread are the usual
accompaniment.

Perdiz con Chocolate
(Spanish Partridge in Chocolate Sauce)

2 young partridges
1 square unsweetened
   chocolate, chopped
1 onion chopped
6 cloves of garlic, one pierced
   with a whole clove
1 bay leaf
3 tablespoons olive oil
2 cups red wine
¼ cup red wine vinegar
salt and pepper
2 tablespoons fresh white
   breadcrumbs
small boiled new potatoes
   (for serving)

Trussing needle and string

Method
Truss the partridges.

   In a flameproof casserole
put the onion, garlic, bay leaf,
oil, wine, vinegar, chocolate
and seasoning. Heat gently
until the chocolate melts, then
put in the partridges.

   Cover the pot, baste the
birds occasionally, and simmer over low heat or bake in
a moderate oven (350°F) for
50–60 minutes or until the
partridges are tender.

   Remove trussing strings,
transfer the partridges to a
platter and keep warm.

   Strain the sauce, stir in the
breadcrumbs and cook, stirring, until slightly thickened.
Taste for seasoning, spoon a
little of the sauce over the
partridges and serve the rest
separately. Garnish the platter
with small boiled new potatoes.

DESSERTS

The Arabs ruled a large part of
the Iberian peninsula for more
than 400 years and left their
mark on the cooking in the
love of sweet cakes and desserts. The favorite is flan —
a rich caramel custard — and
Portugal offers a range of nut-
flavored cakes and creams,
usually based on egg yolk.

   Almonds are enjoyed everywhere and many of the traditional cakes made with them
are convent specialties,
offered to visitors. However,
cakes and sweetmeats are
most often enjoyed as morning or afternoon snacks.

   Fruit is the usual end to a
meal, such as sunripened
Spanish melons, freshly
picked figs and the famous
sweet oranges.

Churros
(Spanish Crullers)

½ cup milk
½ cup water
pinch of salt
1 cup flour
1 egg, beaten to mix
deep fat (for frying)
granulated sugar (for
   sprinkling)

*Churros tube or cookie press,
fitted with a star disc*

In Spain these crullers are
usually eaten with hot coffee
or chocolate for breakfast.
The crullers are forced through
a special tube into hot deep
fat so they form 10–12 inch
lengths that curl up and puff
to about 1 inch in diameter.
They are sprinkled with sugar
before serving. Makes about
twelve 4 inch churros.

Method
Heat the milk and water with
the salt until just boiling.
Take from the heat and add
the flour all at once. Immediately beat until the mixture is
smooth and comes away from
the sides of the pan. Gradually
beat in the egg.

   Put the mixture into a churros tube or cookie press fitted
with a star disc.

   Heat the deep fat to 375°F
on a fat thermometer and pipe
the mixture into the hot fat in a
spiral. Fry until golden brown
and drain on paper towels.
Fry the remaining mixture
in the same way.

   Cut the churros in 4–5 inch
lengths and sprinkle with
sugar before serving.

Pipe cruller mixture into the hot deep fat in a spiral and fry until it is golden brown

For churros, put cruller mixture into a churros tube or cookie press, fitted with a star disc

Buñuelos de Viento
(All Saints' Day Fritters)

½ cup water
½ cup milk
2 tablespoons sugar
pinch of salt
1 tablespoon brandy
⅓ cup lard
1 cup flour
grated rind of 1 lemon
3 large eggs
deep fat (for frying)
granulated or confectioners'
    sugar (for sprinkling)

Buñuelo in Spanish means fritter. The simplest ones, often sold outdoors, are made of yeast dough cut in a circle like doughnuts and deep fried. Other savory fritters are filled with fish, ham or eggs and sweet ones are often made with fruit. The following recipe is traditional on All Saints' Day. Makes 50–60 buñuelos.

Method
In a pan heat the water, milk, sugar, salt, brandy and lard until the lard is melted. Bring just to a boil, take from the heat and add all the flour with the lemon rind. Immediately beat until the mixture is smooth and comes away from the sides of the pan. Add the eggs, one by one, beating well after each addition. Beat the mixture for 1 minute after adding the last egg.

Drop teaspoonsful of the mixture into hot deep fat (350°F on a fat thermometer) and fry a few buñuelos at a time, increasing the heat to 375°F so they swell as much as possible.

When golden brown, drain the fritters on paper towels and fry the remaining mixture in the same way. Let cool and sprinkle with sugar before serving.

If you like, buñuelos can be split and filled with 1 cup heavy cream, stiffly whipped, or with vanilla pastry cream.

Churros, cut in small lengths and sprinkled with sugar, are popular for breakfast with hot chocolate

Flan
(Caramel Custard)

3 cups milk
pared rind of 1 lemon
1 cinnamon stick
4 eggs
4 egg yolks
¾ cup sugar

For caramel
¾ cup sugar
⅓ cup water

Soufflé or baking dish (5 cup capacity)

Flan is the favorite dessert in both Spain and Portugal.

Method
Scald the milk with the lemon rind and cinnamon stick and let stand in a warm place for 15 minutes to infuse.

To make the caramel: heat the sugar in the water until it is dissolved, then boil the mixture without stirring until a deep golden caramel. Take the caramel from the heat, at once pour it into the soufflé or baking dish and tilt and rotate the dish so the sides are lined with caramel.

Beat the eggs and egg yolks with the sugar until thoroughly mixed, and stir in the hot milk. Strain the mixture into the caramel-lined dish and set it in a water bath. Bake in a moderate oven (350°F) for 40–50 minutes or until a knife inserted near the center comes out clean. Let cool in the dish.

A short time before serving, loosen the sides of the flan with a knife and turn it out into a flat serving dish with a rim.

Flan de Naranja
(Spanish Orange Flan)

2½ cups orange juice
grated rind of 1 orange
8 eggs
1 cup sugar

For caramel
¾ cup sugar
⅓ cup water

Baking or soufflé dish (1½ quart capacity)

Method
To make the caramel: heat the sugar in the water until it is dissolved, then boil the mixture without stirring until it is a deep golden caramel. Take the caramel from the heat, at once pour it into the baking or soufflé dish and tilt and rotate the dish to coat the sides.

Beat the eggs with the sugar until light and slightly thickened. Stir in the orange juice and strain the mixture. Stir in the orange rind and pour the mixture into the prepared dish. Set the dish in a water bath and bake in a moderate oven (350°F) for 40–50 minutes or until a knife inserted near the center comes out clean. Let cool in the dish.

A short time before serving, loosen the sides of the mold with a knife and turn it out onto a platter with a lid.

Arroz con Leche
(Spanish Rice Pudding)

½ cup rice
2½–3 cups milk
vanilla bean or 1 teaspoon vanilla extract
1 tablespoon butter
½ cup sugar
ground cinnamon (for sprinkling)

Method
Scald the rice by pouring it slowly into boiling water, boiling for 3 minutes, then draining it.

Bring 2½ cups milk to a boil with the vanilla bean, if using, gradually add the rice and bring back to a boil. Do not add the vanilla extract at this point. Cover and cook over very low heat for about 30 minutes, stirring occasionally. If the rice is dry, add more milk and simmer 10–15 minutes longer or until the rice is tender.

Stir in the butter and sugar, cover and let the rice cool to tepid. It should be thick but still drop fairly easily from the spoon; if necessary, add more milk. Discard the vanilla bean or, if using vanilla extract, add it now and pour the rice into a serving bowl. Chill and sprinkle with ground cinnamon before serving.

Arroz con Leche a la Gallega
(Galician Rice Pudding)

Make arroz con leche as above, infusing the milk with 3-inch cinnamon stick as well as the vanilla bean, and pour it into a shallow baking dish. Sprinkle it thickly with sugar and broil until the sugar caramelizes. Let the caramel cool.

If you like, when serving, pour a few tablespoons of red wine over the rice pudding in individual bowls.

Pan Dulce
(Spanish Sweet Bread)

1 cup flour
½ teaspoon salt
6 eggs, separated
1 cup sugar
grated rind of 1 lemon
¼ cup raisins
¼ cup mixed chopped candied peel

Large loaf pan (9 X 5 X 3 inches)

An Italian version of this sweet bread was given in Volume 13.

Method
Set the oven at moderate (350°F) and grease and flour the loaf pan. Sift the flour with the salt.

Beat the egg yolks with the sugar until thick and light. Stiffly whip the egg whites and fold them into the egg yolk mixture in 3 batches alternately with the flour. Lastly, fold in the lemon rind, raisins and candied peel.

Spoon the mixture into the prepared loaf pan and bake in the heated oven for about 1 hour or until a skewer inserted in the bread comes out clean. Transfer the loaf to a wire rack to cool.

Brazo de Gitano
(Gipsy's Arm Cake)

½ cup flour
pinch of salt
4 eggs, separated
½ cup sugar

For filling
1½ cups milk
1 vanilla bean, split
3 egg yolks
3 tablespoons sugar
2 tablespoons cornstarch
¼ cup dark rum
confectioners' sugar (for sprinkling)

11 X 15 inch jelly roll pan

Method
Set oven at moderate (350°F). Grease the jelly roll pan, line the base with a rectangle of wax paper, grease it and sprinkle the pan with sugar, then with flour and discard excess.

To make jelly roll: sift the flour with the salt. Beat the egg yolks with the sugar until thick and light. Stiffly whip the egg whites and fold into the yolk mixture alternately with the sifted flour. Spread the batter in the prepared pan and bake in the heated oven for 12–15 minutes or until the edges are lightly browned.

Turn out the jelly roll onto a dish towel or sheet of wax paper sprinkled with confectioners' sugar. Quickly but carefully remove the rectangle of wax paper, trim the edges of the cake to give a neat finish and remove the browned edges, and roll up tightly with the towel or wax paper inside; let cool.

To make the filling: scald the milk with the vanilla bean, cover the pan and let stand in a warm place to infuse for 10 minutes. Beat the egg yolks with the sugar until slightly thickened and stir in the cornstarch. Strain in the hot milk, stir well and return to the pan. Bring to a boil, stirring until thickened, and simmer 2 minutes. Take from the heat, cover and let cool; beat in the rum.

Carefully unroll the jelly roll and remove the towel or paper. Spread the inside with the rum-flavored pastry cream, roll up the cake and sprinkle with confectioners' sugar.

Toucinho do Céu
(Portuguese 'Bacon from Heaven' Cake)

2 cups whole blanched almonds, ground
2 cups sugar
¾ cup water
8 egg yolks
grated rind of ½ lemon
1 teaspoon almond extract

For topping
¼ cup slivered almonds
¼ cup granulated sugar

8 inch springform pan

Method
Set oven at moderate (350°F); grease the springform pan and sprinkle it with sugar, discarding the excess.

In a saucepan heat the sugar in the water until it is dissolved, then boil until the syrup forms a thread between the finger and thumb when a little is lifted on a spoon (234°F on a sugar thermometer). Add the ground almonds and cook, stirring constantly, for 5 minutes or until the mixture becomes slightly clear. Let cool slightly.

Beat the egg yolks until thick and light, then gradually beat in the warm almond mixture. Continue beating until cool and thick. Add the lemon rind and almond extract and cook over very low heat, stirring, for 5–10 minutes or until the mixture thickens enough to make a ribbon trail when the spoon is lifted.

Transfer the mixture to the prepared pan. Sprinkle with slivered almonds, then with granulated sugar and bake in the heated oven for 40–45 minutes or until a skewer inserted in the center comes out clean. Let the cake cool to tepid in the pan, then transfer it to a platter and serve warm or at room temperature. Cut into wedges to serve.

Croquetes com Amendoas
(Portuguese Almond Croquettes)

1½ cups whole blanched almonds, ground
2 egg whites
½ cup sugar
1 cup cake crumbs
¼ cup port
grated rind of ½ orange

For coating
2 egg yolks
2 teaspoons water
1 cup dry white breadcrumbs
2–3 tablespoons confectioners' sugar (for sprinkling)
deep fat (for frying)

Makes about 24 croquettes.

Method
Stiffly beat the egg whites, add the sugar gradually and continue beating for 2–3 minutes until the mixture is glossy. Stir in the ground almonds and cake crumbs alternately with the port, then add the orange rind.

Shape the mixture into walnut-sized balls and coat them with the egg yolks, beaten to mix with the water. Roll the balls in breadcrumbs and sprinkle them with confectioners' sugar. Fry them, a few at a time, in hot deep fat (375°F on a fat thermometer) and drain well on paper towels. Serve the croquettes hot or cold.

Spanish and Portuguese cooking

Typical Portuguese desserts using almonds are 'Bacon from Heaven' cake and croquettes

Petits fours are (from the top): fours aux amandes, colettes, rochers aux amandes, salambos (topped with caramel and chopped pistachios), coquettes au café and chocolate-topped cream puffs

HOW TO MAKE PETITS FOURS

Petits fours are melting little pastries and their appearance is half their charm. They can be based on meringue, choux pastry, sponge cake coated with icing or sweet pastry, or they may be tiny cookies made with a rich dough. No matter how they are made, petits fours should always be easy to eat in one mouthful, their flavor must be concentrated because of their size and they must have a colorful decoration. For a professional finish, set them in paper cases and be sure to make them all the same size.

Serve petits fours instead of dessert after an elaborate meal because they are delicious with coffee or, if you like, make them for a buffet or afternoon reception.

Fours aux Amandes

$\frac{2}{3}$ cup whole blanched almonds, ground
$\frac{1}{3}$ cup sugar
2 egg whites
$\frac{1}{2}$ teaspoon vanilla or
$\frac{1}{4}$ teaspoon almond extract
few blanched almonds, split in half or candied cherries, cut in quarters (for decoration)

For glaze
1 tablespoon sugar
2 tablespoons milk

Silicone paper; pastry bag and large star tube

Makes 12–14 petits fours.

Method
Set oven at moderate (350°F) and line a baking sheet with silicone paper.

Mix the almonds and sugar and sift them through a coarse strainer. Beat egg whites until they hold a stiff peak and fold in the almonds and sugar with vanilla or almond flavoring.

Spoon the mixture into the pastry bag fitted with the star tube and pipe flowers, rosettes or figure eights onto the lined baking sheet. Decorate with split almonds or pieces of candied cherry and bake in heated oven for 15 minutes or until just beginning to brown.

To make the glaze: heat the sugar with the milk until dissolved and brush over the petits fours while still hot. Cool and peel off the paper before they are completely cold.

Coquettes au Café

2 egg white quantity of meringue cuite (see right)
1 tablespoon dry instant coffee (or to taste)
4–5 candied cherries, cut in quarters

Pastry bag and $\frac{1}{4}$ inch plain tube

Makes 16 petits fours.

Method
Set oven at moderately low (325°F) and grease and flour a baking sheet.

Prepare the meringue cuite and stir in instant coffee to taste. Spoon the mixture into the pastry bag fitted with the $\frac{1}{4}$ inch tube and pipe small meringues onto the prepared baking sheet, reserving about one-quarter of the mixture in the bag.

Bake the meringues in the heated oven for 18–20 minutes or until crisp. Transfer to a wire rack to cool, then sandwich them with the remaining meringue mixture. Top each with a piece of candied cherry.

Rochers aux Amandes
(Almond Rocks)

2 egg white quantity of meringue cuite (see right)
6 tablespoons slivered almonds
1 teaspoon vanilla or
2 teaspoons dry instant coffee or 1 square (1 oz) unsweetened chocolate (melted over hot water)

Makes 30–32 petits fours.

Method
Set oven at moderate (350°F); grease and flour a baking sheet.

Prepare the meringue cuite and fold in the almonds and flavoring. Shape small mounds with 2 teaspoons on the prepared baking sheet and bake in heated oven for 8–10 minutes or until the rochers are firm on the outside.

Meringue Cuite

2 cups confectioners' sugar
4 egg whites
1 teaspoon vanilla

This quantity of meringue cuite is enough to make the coquettes au café and rochers aux amandes recipes.

Method
Sift the confectioners' sugar through a fine sieve onto a sheet of wax paper; if beating by hand, have ready a pan half full of gently simmering water.

Beat the egg whites with a rotary or electric beater until frothy. Beat in the confectioners' sugar 1 teaspoon at a time, and when all has been added beat in the vanilla. If beating by hand, set the bowl over hot water and continue beating until the mixture will hold its shape. No heat is needed if using an electric beater.

To test, lift a little of the mixture on the beater. If it is ready, it will form a stiff, tall peak.

Salambos

4–5 egg quantity of choux pastry (see Volume 6)
$\frac{3}{4}$ cup sugar (for caramel topping)
2–3 tablespoons finely chopped pistachios

For orange cream
1 orange
4–6 cubes of sugar
1 teaspoon rum or brandy (optional)
$1\frac{1}{2}$ cups heavy cream, whipped until it holds a soft shape

Pastry bag and $\frac{3}{8}$ inch and small plain tubes

This is a variation of the traditional salambos that are filled with pastry cream flavored with kirsch and then topped with icing.

Method
Set oven at hot (400°F).

Prepare the choux pastry dough. Pipe it out into small $1–1\frac{1}{2}$ inch mounds, fairly far apart on dampened baking sheets. Bake 10 minutes in the heated oven, then raise the temperature to 425°F and bake for 10–20 minutes longer. When the salambos are crisp, prick the sides to release the steam and cool them on a wire rack.

To make the caramel topping: put the sugar in a small, heavy-based pan and cook slowly until it melts and forms a rich brown syrup.

Watchpoint: immediately stop the caramel cooking by dipping the bottom of the pan in warm water.

Dip the top of each salambo quickly into the caramel while it is still warm and liquid, then into the chopped pistachios.

To make the orange cream: rub the sugar cubes over the orange rind to remove all the zest (the oil in orange rind),

132

then crush the cubes and mix with a little juice from the orange to make a rich syrup. Add rum or brandy if you like. Gradually beat the orange syrup into the whipped cream. **Watchpoint:** add this syrup carefully because the whipped cream can curdle if it is beaten too much.

Make slits in the sides of the salambos and fill them with the orange cream, preferably using a pastry bag fitted with a small plain tube.

Alternatively, dip the puffs into melted semisweet chocolate, and then into browned slivered almonds.

Orangines

⅓ cup finely chopped candied orange peel
6 tablespoons flour
¼ cup butter
¼ cup sugar
½ cup finely chopped blanched almonds
2 teaspoons milk
1—2 drops of red food coloring

Makes 24 petits fours.

Method
Set oven at moderate (350°F) and grease a baking sheet.

Sift the flour. Cream the butter, gradually add the sugar and beat until light and fluffy. Stir in the almonds, candied peel, flour, milk and food coloring.
Watchpoint: color the mixture very delicately with only 1—2 drops of coloring.

Drop the mixture a teaspoon at a time on the baking sheet, leaving plenty of space between each spoonful. Flatten with a wet fork and bake in heated oven for 10—12 minutes or until brown around the edges.
Watchpoint: bake only one spoonful of mixture at first to

test for size — they should be no more than 2 inches in diameter.

Leave the orangines for 2—3 minutes so they are almost firm before lifting from the baking sheet.

Colettes

2 squares (2 oz) semisweet chocolate, coarsely chopped
few chopped pistachios (for decoration) – optional

For ganache cream
2½ squares (2½ oz) semisweet chocolate, coarsely chopped
1 tablespoon unsalted butter
¼ cup heavy cream
2 teaspoons rum

10—12 foil or paper candy cases; pastry bag and a small star tube

Makes 10—12 petits fours.

Method
Melt the 2 squares of chopped chocolate on a heatproof plate over a pan of hot water. Work with a metal spatula as the chocolate melts and do not let it get too hot or it will lose its gloss; leave until cool but still soft. Dip the end of a finger into the chocolate and line the cases. Chill until hard.

To make the ganache cream: melt the chocolate in a pan with the butter and cream. Cook until the mixture is thick, beating well. Add rum and let cool.
Watchpoint: if the mixture separates, stir in a few drops of cold water.

When the chocolate cases are firm, remove the foil or paper and fill with ganache cream, using a pastry bag fitted with a star tube. Decorate with small pieces of pistachio.

Fondant pretzels are sprinkled with confectioners' sugar

Fondant Pretzels

1 cup flour
pinch of salt
pinch of ground aniseed or ½ teaspoon ground cinnamon
5 tablespoons butter
1 tablespoon sugar
1 egg
confectioners' sugar (for sprinkling)

Makes 14 petits fours.

Method
Set oven at hot (400°F) and grease a baking sheet.

Sift the flour with the salt and flavoring onto a work top or pastry board, make a well in the center and add the butter, sugar and egg. Work these ingredients to a paste with the fingertips, then draw in the flour with the whole hand to form a smooth dough, as for French flan pastry. Chill 30 minutes.

Divide the dough into even

walnut-sized pieces and roll into cylinders on a floured board so that each piece is the thickness of a little finger. Twist into the traditional pretzel knot, sticking the ends together with a little water.

Place on the prepared baking sheet and bake in heated oven for 7—8 minutes or until just beginning to brown. Take pretzels from the oven and while still hot sprinkle with confectioners' sugar.

Petit fours take their name from the small ovens in which they were originally baked. These came into use in the mid-17th century when La Varenne, the famous French pâtissier, recommended that cooks use them for baking small quantities of pastries.

Cooking Curiosities

When is an artichoke not an artichoke? When it's a Jerusalem artichoke, which looks like a potato and is a member of the sunflower family. Although it is a root, with no leaves or choke, it does have a similar flavor to the globe artichoke. And Jerusalem artichokes have nothing to do with the holy city; their name is a corruption of the Italian word for a type of sunflower called 'girasole'.

Jerusalem artichokes were first discovered in Massachusetts in 1605 by the explorer Champlain and they have been known here since the American Indians cultivated them in the early 17th century.

Jerusalem artichokes are white-fleshed roots with a crisp texture. To prepare them, wash and scrub them thoroughly, then pare, if you like, and bake, steam, boil or fry them. They are available in specialty markets from October to March.

Globe artichoke

© Mary Evans Picture Library

Jerusalem artichoke

135

INDEX
(Volume 16)

A

All Saints' Day fritters 125
Almond(s)
  croquettes 128
  petits fours 132–133
  Portuguese cake 128
  rocks 132
Anchovy butter 76
Apricot jam (dried) 97
Arroz con leche (Spanish rice pudding) 127
Arroz con leche a la Gallega (Galician rice pudding) 127
Artichoke(s)
  hearts, to prepare 72
  salad with tomatoes 72
  stuffed vinaigrette 10
Aspic, quick 42
Austrian rum cake 39

B

Bacalao a la Vizcaina (Basque salt cod) 120
Bacalhau Portuguêsa (Portuguese salt cod) 121
'Bacon and heaven' cake 128
Bacon and spinach salad 68
Ballotines of chicken with prunes 106
Bamboo shoot fan (garnish) 48
Banderillas (miniature kebabs) 112
Bangkok chicken 30

Basque cooking
  fish stew 120
  Salt cod 120
Bean (white), Galician soup 115
Bean paste bun (Hikichamanju) 57
Beef
  carbonade of 33
  roulade 66
  steak
    fillet (Marchand de vin) 61
    roulades with celery stuffing 31
Bell peppers, to prepare 114
Brazo de Gitano (Gipsy's Arm cake) 128
Bread, Spanish sweet 127
Broth (dashi) 49
Buffet, poolside 66
Bun, bean paste (Hikichamanju) 57
Bunuelos de Viento 125
Butter
  anchovy 76
  to clarify 62

C

Cabbage crêpes (stuffed) 33
Cacik (yogurt soup) 106
Cake(s), large
  Portuguese 'bacon and heaven' cake 128
  rum, Austrian 39
Calamondin preserves 97
Caldeirada (Portuguese fisherman's stew) 119
Caldo gallego (Galician white bean soup) 115
Caldo verde (Portuguese kale soup) 116

Caramel
  custard 127
  pecan mousse, iced 72
Carbonade
  of beef 33
  definition 33
Carrot(s), preparation of (Japanese cooking) 57
Catalan shrimps (Langostinos a la Catalana) 114
Cauliflower
  in garlic mayonnaise (coliflor con ali-oli) 114
  mold 84
Celery
  stuffing 31
  vinegar 100
Chantilly cream 15
Charlotte, strawberry 36
Chawan mushi 52
Cheese straws 70
Cheese, with veal 30
Chestnut parfait 35
Chicken
  ballotines of, with prunes 106
  Bangkok 30
  in custard (Chawan mushi) 52
  molds 89
    liver 90
  mousseline 91
  Portuguese, with rice 122
  quenelles 91
  rolls, with tongue 30
  sashi 52
  Spanish, with ham and peppers 122
  spiced 29, 52
  à la Suisse 12
  terrine of 29
  tuna 79
Chili vinegar 101
Chocolate squares 105
Chorizo sausage
  definition 116
  with lentil purée 114

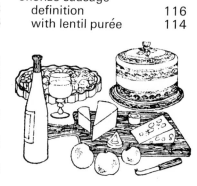

Choux pastry, in salambos 132
Chrysanthemum turnips 57
Churros (Spanish crullers) 124
Cocido Madrileño (Madrid meat, fowl and vegetable soup) 122
Coconut milk 22
Cod, Basque salt 120
  Portuguese 121
Colettes 133
Coliflor con ali-oli (cauliflower in garlic mayonnaise) 114

Cooking for a freezer 25–39
Cooking outdoors 59–73
Coquettes au café 132
Corn in the husk (roasted) 62
Court bouillon, for shellfish 18
Crab armoricaine 21
Crab croquettes 21
Crêpes farcies au chou (stuffed cabbage crêpes) 33
Croquettes
  almond 128
  crab 21
Cucumber vinegar 100
Curried shrimps 22

D

Daikon (white radish) 57
Dashi (broth) 49
Demi-glace sauce 90
Drinks, sangrià 68
Duck, terrine of 29
Duxelles sauce 84

E

Eggplant
  mold 84
  provençale 68
Eggs
  Maryland 42
  plum flower 58
Empanadillas (miniature
    turnovers) 112
  fillings for 112

F

Fish
  balls with tomato sauce 87
  molds 85–87
    individual 85
    Newburg 87
    salmon 85
    tomato 87
  mousseline 91
  quenelles 91
  in seaweed with
    vinegared rice
    (Norimaki sushi) 50
  sliced raw (sashimi) 51
  stew 119, 120
  stock 22
Fisherman's stew,
  Portuguese 119

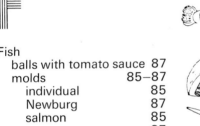

Flan
  caramel custard 127
  de Naranja 127
  peach, fresh 68
  Spanish orange 127
  steak 109

Flower petals, garnish 48
Fondant pretzels 133
Fours aux amandes 132
Frango Portuguêsa
  (Portuguese chicken
    with rice) 122
Freezer, cooking for 25–39
Fried rice 44
Frozen foods, to thaw 27
Fruit
  marinated 44
  purée, to freeze 39
  in strawberry cream 39

G

Galette Normande 80
Galician cooking
  rice pudding 127
  white bean soup 115
Ganache cream 133
Gardener's omelet 116
Garlic
  mayonnaise 114
  soup, Spanish 115
Garnish, for soup 48
Gazpacho
  alicantina 115
  definition 115
Ginger and rhubarb jam 96
Gipsy's Arm cake 128
Girls' festival (definition) 57
Grapefruit marmalade 96
Grape jam, green 96
Green soup (potage vert) 77

H

Ham
  with chicken and
    peppers 122
  mold 88
  serraño 115
Hikichamanju (bean paste
    bun) 57
Hors d'oeuvre
  cocktail party 130
  Spanish and Portuguese
    cooking 112
Horseradish vinegar 101
Hot savory molds 83–91

I J

Ice cream, peppermint 35
Iced caramel pecan mouse 72

Jam
  apricot, dried 97
  green grape 96
  pineapple 96
  rhubarb and ginger 96
Japanese cooking 47–58
  ingredients 48
  soup garnishes 48–49
Jell point 94
Jelly
  lime 97
  orange lemon 97

K

Kakimiso (oyster soup) 49
Kale soup 116
Kebabs, miniature
    (banderillas) 112
Kumquat preserves 97

L

Lamb chops with mushroom
    stuffing 62
Langosta a la Barcelonese
  (spiny lobster from
    Barcelona) 119
Langostinos a la Catalana
  (Catalan shrimps) 114
Leaves (vegetable), as a
    garnish 48
Leek and rice soup 104
Lemon orange jelly 97
Lemon pine needles
    (garnish) 48
Lentil purée with chorizo
    sausage 114
Lime
  garnish 48
  jelly 97
Linguica sausage 116
Liver (chicken) omelet 116
Lobster
  Americaine 21
  boréale 19
  margareta 18
  pilaf 18
  spiny 119
Luting paste 29

M

Madère sauce 90
Madrid meat, fowl and vegetable stew 122
Mancha vegetable stew 119
Marchand de vin (fillet steak) 61
Marinated fruit bowl 44
Marmalade
  orange 1 and 2 94
  pineapple and grapefruit 96
  tangerine 95
  three fruit 95
Mayonnaise, garlic 114
Mejillones gratinados (browned mussel) 114
Meringue cuite 132
Mint vinegar 100
Misoshiru (soybean paste soup) 49

Molds
  hot savory 83–91
  to steam 84
  to turn out 84
  in a water bath 84
Mousse
  caramel pecan, iced 72
  tangerine 104
Mousseline
  definition 91
  of fish, chicken, rabbit or veal 91
Mushroom
  cream sauce 91
  garnish 48
  stuffing, with lamb chops 62
  in white wine 76
Mussels, browned (Mejillones gratinados) 114
Mustard sauce
  cream 30
  simple 21

N

Newburg, fish mold 87
New Year (Japanese) 58
Norimaki sushi (vinegared rice and fish in seaweed) 50
Normande galette 80

O

Omelet
  shredded 51
  tortilla 116
Onigari-yaki (broiled shrimps in soy sauce) 57
Onions, broiled 62
Orange
  cream 132
  flan 127
  jelly with lemons 97
  lemon jelly 97
  marmalade 1 and 2 94
Orangines 133
Outdoor entertaining 59–73
Oyster soup (kakimiso) 49

P

Paella 120
  definition 120
Paella Valenciana 120
Pan dulce (Spanish sweet bread) 127
Panada 87
Parfait, chestnut 35
Partridge in chocolate sauce 124
Paste, luting 29
Pastry, Danish shortcake 80
Pâté, smoked tongue 66
Peach
  flan 68
  melba 15
  definition 15
Pears en douillon (pears in a sleeve) 36
Pears in redcurrant jelly 64
Pecans, in iced caramel mousse 72
Pectin (definition) 96
Peppermint ice cream 35
Peppers
  bell, to prepare 114
  with chicken and ham 122
Perdiz con Chocolate (Spanish Partridge in chocolate sauce) 124
Petits fours 130–133
  definition 133
Pie, seafood 21
Pilaf, lobster 18
Pineapple
  jam 96
  marmalade, with grapefruit 96
Pisto 119
  definition 119
Pisto Manchego (La Manga vegetable stew) 119
Plum flower egg 58
Pollo chilindrón (Spanish chicken with ham and peppers) 122
Porco Alentejana (Portuguese pork with clams) 124
Pork
  chops with tomato sauce 30
  with clams 124
  tenderloin, spiced 44

Portuguese cooking 111–129
Potage
  pondicherry 104
  vert (green soup) 77
Potato
  omelet 116
  refrigerator rolls 39
  à la Suisse 62
Praline cream 107
Preparation of vegetables 57
Preserves 93–97
  to skim and store 94
  to test for jell 94
Pretzels, fondant 133
Prunes with ballotines of chicken 106
Purée (fruit), to freeze 39

Q R

Quenelles 91
  without molds 91
  to poach 91
Quick aspic 42

Rabbit
  mousseline of 91
  quenelles 91
Radish
  pickled (Japanese) 54
  white (daikon) 57
Ragoût of lamb 31
Raspberry vinegar 100
Refrigerator rolls 39
Rhubarb and ginger jam 96
Rice
  chicken with 122
  fried 44
  pudding (Spanish) 127
  soup
    Japanese cake 58
    with leeks 104

Rice *continued*
vinegared 51
and fish in seaweed
(Norimaki sushi) 50
Rochers aux amandes
(almond rocks) 132
Rolls
potato refrigerator 39
small, to heat 77
Rose petal vinegar 101
Roulades
beef 66
steak, with celery
stuffing 31
Rum cake, Austrian 39

S

Salad
spinach and bacon 68
tomato and artichoke 72
zucchini 109
Salambos 132
Salmon mold 85
Sangria 68
Sardine omelet 116
Sashimi 51
definition 48
Sauce
demi-glace 90
duxelles 84
madère 90
mushroom cream 91
mustard
cream 30
simple 20
périgueux 90
suprême 90
tomato 30
tuna 104
velouté 88
Sausage
chorizo 114, 116
linguica 116
Scallions, preparation of 57
Scallops paimpolaise 23
Seafood pie 27
Seaweed, vinegared rice
and fish in (Norimaki
sushi) 50
Serraño ham 115
Sesame seeds with
spinach 52

Shallot vinegar 101
Shellfish 16–23
sushi 58
Sherbet, tangerine 35
Shoyu (definition) 48
Shrimps
broiled in soy sauce 57
curried 22
garnish 48
gourmet 22
Simple mustard sauce 21
Sliced raw fish 51
Sopa de ajo (Spanish garlic
soup) 115
Soup
bean, Galician white 115
cream of leek and rice 104
garlic 115
garnish 48
gazpacho alicantina 115
green 77
kale 116
oyster 49
rice cake 58
soybean paste
(Misoshivu) 49
watercress, chilled 70
yogurt (cacik) 106
Soybean paste soup 49
Soy sauce (Japanese)
definition 48
with broiled shrimps
(Onigari-yaki) 57
Spanish cooking 111–129
Spareribs, spiced 61
Spiced chicken 29
pork 44
tangerine 97
vinegar 101
Spinach
salad, with bacon 68
with sesame 52
Squabs, stuffed en cocotte
with olives 70
Squid, to clean 119
Steak
fillet (Marchand de vin) 61
flan 109
roulades with celery
stuffing 31
Stew (Portuguese and
Spanish cooking)
119, 120, 122
Stock, fish 22
Strawberry
cardinal 109
charlotte 36
cream in fruit 39

Stuffed artichokes
vinaigrette 10
Stuffed squabs en cocotte
with olives 70
Stuffing, celery 31
Sukiyaki 54
Summer vinegar 100
Suprême sauce 90
Sushi
Norimaki (vinegared rice
and fish in seaweed) 50
shellfish 58
Sweetbreads
to prepare 12
tante Marie 12
Sweet Bread (Spanish) 125

T

Tangerine
marmalade 95
mousse 104
sherbet 35
spiced 97
Tante Marie sweetbreads 12
Tapas 112
Tarragon vinegar 100
Tempura 52
definition 48
Terrine
of chicken 29
of duck 29
Thaw frozen foods 27
Tomato
and artichoke salad 72
fish mold 87
paste 84
provençale 62
sauce 30
simple 87
vinegar 101
Tongue
pâté, smoked 66
rolls, with chicken 30
Torisashi (chicken sashi) 52
Tortilla (omelet) 116
Balear 116
basic 116
Granadina 116
a la Jardinera 116
Toucinho do céu (Portuguese
'bacon and heaven'
cake) 128

Tuna
with chicken 79
sauce 104
Turnips, chrysanthemum 57
Turnovers, miniature
(empanadillas) 112

VW

Veal
chasseur 31
with cheese 30
mold 89
mousseline 91
quenelles 91
sauté 91
tuna sauce 104
Vegetable stew 119
Velouté sauce 88
Vinegar, homemade 99–101
Vitello tonnato (veal with
tuna sauce) 104

Watercress soup, chilled 70
Watermelon rafraîchis 64
White wine with
mushrooms 76
Wrap cooked dishes 27

YZ

Yogurt soup (cacik) 106

Zarzuela (Basque fish
stew) 120
Zoni (rice cake soup) 58
Zucchini
mold 85
salad 109

Acknowledgments
Photographs by Fred J. Maroon on pages 16, 28, 34, 46, 49, 50, 53, 55 and 56. Photographs by Ross Chapple on pages 60, 65, 67, 69, 73, 110, 113, 118, 125, 126 and 129; styling by Fay Abell. Photograph on page 24, courtesy of Reynolds Metals Co. Other photographs by Michael Leale, John Cowderoy and John Ledger.

NOTES

Notes